THE OTHER STATE
New Mexico, USA

SILENT NIGHT, HOLY NIGHT —N.M.

THE OTHER STATE
New Mexico, USA

Richard McCord

SUNSTONE
PRESS

SANTA FE

Cover Illustration by Lisa T. Bemis
"Silent Night, Holy Night—New Mexico"

Sunstone books may be purchased for educational, business, or sales
promotional use. For information please write: Special Markets Department,
Sunstone Press, P.O. Box 2321, Santa Fe, New Mexico 87504-2321.

Library of Congress Cataloging-in-Publication Data

McCord, Richard,
   The other state : New Mexico, USA / by Richard McCord.
     p. cm.
   ISBN 0-86534-403-5 (softcover)
   1. New Mexico—Description and travel—Anecdotes. 2. New Mexico—Social
life and customs—Anecdotes. 3. McCord, Richard—Anecdotes.
4. Santa Fe (N.M.)—Biography—Anecdotes. 5. Santa Fe (N.M.)—Social life
and customs—Anecdotes. I. Title.
F801.2 .M38 2003
978.9—dc21

                              2003013651

Published in

SUNSTONE PRESS
POST OFFICE BOX 2321
SANTA FE, NM 87504-2321 / USA
(505) 988-4418 / ORDERS ONLY (800) 243-5644
FAX (505) 988-1025
WWW.SUNSTONEPRESS.COM

To New Mexico and Santa Fe,
which made a place for me.

Contents

PART I

The Storyteller

The First Time

*F*light 297 from Chicago to Albuquerque hit turbulent air over the Sangre de Cristo Mountains, and the seat-belt light flashed on. I put aside my magazine and gazed down at the 12,000-foot peaks, white with snow. We would be landing in 10 minutes, and I would just look out the window till then.

"How odd," I mused. "I've just spent three winter weeks in the northland—Minnesota, Wisconsin, Chicago— yet the only snow I've seen is back home in the Southwest, in the desert, in New Mexico."

"Can you tell me what we're looking at?" asked a voice on my right. She was a pretty, dark-haired young woman, a student perhaps. Until now she had been reading a book.

"Yes, I think so," I replied, pleased that by now I knew the terrain well enough to identify the landmarks 15,000 feet below. "That's Interstate 25 to Santa Fe, and those are the Sangres, of course. The mountains up ahead are the Ortiz."

"No, that's not what I mean," she said. "Can it really be as dry as it looks? Doesn't anything grow? What are those black dots? And where are all the houses?"

"Oh, then you don't live in New Mexico," I deduced.

"No, this is my first trip to the West."

The plane banked. Our wing dipped, and the window opened onto a vast panorama, of desert and mountain, sun and cloud, snow and shadow and rock, engulfing hundreds of square miles. "Oh my God," she gasped. "I've never seen anything like this."

How I envied her. She was on the edge of one of life's truest thrills, which can come only once: The First Time.

Eagerly she stretched across me for a better view. The black dots, I told her, were trees, juniper and piñon. She could not believe they were so far apart. Yes, the ground was as bare as it seemed, I said. It grew only sagebrush and sere grass, as brown in winter as the soil itself. I pointed out an arroyo. After a rain, I said, it would flow like a river.

"I've only heard of these things," she said with appropriate awe. "I've always lived in Boston."

"What will you do in Albuquerque?" I asked, suddenly fretful that she might pass all her visit within the city limits, plunging no deeper into New Mexico than the Old Town tourist district.

"I'm not staying in Albuquerque," she said. "I'm going to a place called Shiprock. Have you heard of it?"

"Shiprock!" I was astonished. "What takes you to Shiprock?"

"I'll be working in the Shiprock hospital for a month. I'm driving straight there from the airport, in a rented car."

"In the Indian Health Service hospital?" I felt the brooding mystery of the vast reservation, as large as West Virginia, in the Four Corners region. "With the Navajo?"

"Yes, that's right. I've learned the Navajo words for hello, please and thank you. But I'm told Shiprock is really different. Just a couple of traffic lights. And so far away from everything. I hear you can't even get television there."

Total immersion. Her first Western experience was going to be total immersion. I tried to put myself in her place for the next four hours, the next 250 miles, of her life. It took my breath away.

Just west of Albuquerque on Interstate 40 she would first meet desolation. It might frighten her, but she would be safe enough. Then the graceful adobe dwellings of Laguna Indian Pueblo would pass to the north. She would cross the tip of the black lava sea called the Malpais, near Grants. Towering red-rock cliffs would see her into Gallup. Then a darker desolation, north to Shiprock. And all of it for the first time.

Yes, I envied her. One of life's truest thrills.

I promised she would feel the looming presence of the black ancient volcano cone called Shiprock long before she reached the town itself. Whatever else you do, I urged, don't miss Monument Valley, across the Utah line. Get a Navajo friend to take you there. And all by yourself some night, just stand under the stars.

"After your month in Shiprock," I said, "you will not be the same. This land will be part of you, and then you'll come back, again and again."

"Oh, I hope so," she said, her eyes bright and ready. "I hope so." But I had no doubt, for I knew.

The Fires of Summer

*D*ays were cool and nights were crisp at the Hyde State Park campground in May of 1971, when I first came to Santa Fe. But there was no water. The city was withering under a second consecutive year of drought, and the streams in the mountains and the taps at the campground had all run dry.

With me at the campsite was Laurie Knowles, who was then my wife and is now a lawyer with the New Mexico Public Defender's Office. Four months behind us was New York City, where we had worked for daily newspapers. We had left New York to go west, looking for adventure and a new life. By the time we reached Santa Fe, we were road-weary and down to our last $500. So we decided to stay the summer, taking odd jobs and playing, before pushing on to a larger city, maybe Denver or San Francisco, and resuming our careers.

We were hired to tend bar and make sandwiches at Santa Fe Downs, a brand-new horse racing track south of town. To save on rent, we went up to Hyde Park at 8,500 feet in the mountains east of town and put up our tent. With the taps dry, we hauled water up in a five-gallon jug, which held enough to meet our needs for two days. The drought was a nuisance, but it was really not our problem, for we were only passing through.

Each day at the Seven-11 we bought the afternoon daily, *The New Mexican,* for a dime, and watched the news of Santa Fe unfold: The mayor appointed a new police chief, who assured angry Hispanos that his officers were not prejudiced against the *barrio.* A murderer escaped from the penitentiary. The film "Red Sky at Morning," by a local author, premiered at one of the city's two movie theaters.

A planned upscale community, Colonias de Santa Fe, was for sale north of town on Tesuque Indian Pueblo land, amid protests that there was not enough water to support its planned golf course, and that such a development was a desecration of the earth. To keep the municipal airport open, city leaders pleaded for passage of an $800,000 bond issue to repave the runways. The voters turned it down. Laurie and I chuckled. Any city willing to drive 60 miles to Albuquerque to catch a plane couldn't be all bad.

But the biggest news story was the drought. Reservoirs were drying up, the water company warned. Unless people cut back on usage voluntarily, mandatory restrictions would have to be imposed. Previous droughts—in 1946, the early '50s, 1961—were invoked by worried officials. Other Santa Feans, however, saw the drought as a blessing in disguise, for it would keep the city from ever getting too big.

June broke blistering-hot. In the pre-dawn hours of June 5 —opening day at Santa Fe Downs—dry lightning sparked a forest fire in the Jemez Mountains to the west. Before it was quelled four days later, it roared across 5,000 acres to become the biggest fire in the history of the Santa Fe National Forest. Some of our campground neighbors helped fight it as "casuals," at $3.45 an hour, and I was jealous of them. This was the kind of adventure I had left New York to find.

Barely a week after the Jemez fire died out, downtown Santa Fe erupted in flames of a different sort. Two Molotov cocktails were hurled into the old federal building across from the cathedral. Damage was limited to one suite of offices, but the governor of the state, an amiable cowpoke named Bruce King, called out the National Guard. Whether the firebombing was a protest of the Vietnam War, a shout of rage from the *barrio,* or something else, King was taking no chances. With grim, helmeted soldiers patrolling the streets, Santa Fe took on the surreal air of an occupied zone.

Meanwhile, the pleas for residents to conserve water rose to a desperate pitch. Lawns were to be watered only once a week. Cars were not to be washed at all. The restrictions were voluntary, but City Hall was drafting a mandatory ordinance, with $100 fines and 90-day jail terms. Without rain, citizens were told, reservoirs would be "dead-dry" by July 31.

On June 27 lightning struck the forest once again, in the mountains east of the village of Pecos. Within one day more timberland went up in flames than the big Jemez fire had claimed over its whole duration. I saw smoke towering into the sky, and drove straight for it in my car. This time I was determined to be a firefighter.

The fire boss signed me on, as half of a chain-saw team. I was issued a bush hook, a miner's helmet with a light, and a plastic-bagged meal to hang from my belt, then was sent out to the fire line. All night long we cut a yard-wide fire break, only feet and sometimes only inches from the flames. At some point I realized that most of the other men were Indians. That was as exciting as the fire.

In the morning we "casuals" were relieved from duty, replaced by professional firefighters flown in from Idaho. Crews from 10 other states would join them, but nothing could halt the spread of the "Cat Fire," as it was dubbed. Lightning then struck again, setting off the "Dog Fire." The two merged. Soon the conflagration had devoured 12,800 acres, and its perimeter was 28 miles long.

A pall of smoke hung over Santa Fe, and as far south as the Sandia Mountains outside Albuquerque. The air at our campground was barely breathable. The rangers decreed that the Santa Fe and Kit Carson national forests would be closed and evacuated the day after the Fourth of July. But two days before that, an all-night rain did what humans were unable to do, and put out the fire at last.

Once the rains came, they were wild and unrelenting. A rockslide ripped open Hyde Park Road, stranding us on the mountain for three days. The feeder water line to the village of Cerrillos washed away. The only bridge to La Cienega village collapsed, cutting off 65 families from the outside world.

Dropping from the sky in torrents, the prayed-for rain ripped into the shrunken reservoirs with such ferocity that the water filled with silt. For weeks, some 8,000 homes on Santa Fe's east side got nothing but mud from their faucets. Three huge tanker trucks were hastily pressed into service, to provide drinking water for beleagured east-siders, who had to bring their own pots and jugs for taking it home.

Then a black bear wandered into town, climbed a tree behind a school, was tranquilized and returned to the wild.

* * *

When the summer of 1971 ended, Laurie and I did not move on as we had planned. *Nowhere else will we find a town as vivid and as vital as this one*, we agreed. We must make a way to stay. We will build our lives here in Santa Fe, in New Mexico.

The Years That Flowed

*N*ow all of that is three decades ago. How quickly the years flowed.

Laurie and I lived in our tent in Hyde Park from May of 1971 until October. We would have stayed longer, but one morning the campground was covered with snow and our fingers were too cold to cook breakfast on the Coleman Stove. For $65 a month we rented a little house in the village of Tesuque from Jesse Cordova, a soft-spoken Hispanic gentleman who during Prohibition years had smuggled booze north from Mexico in his Model T. Upon leaving the campground we presented the chief park ranger with a bottle of fine Scotch whisky, in appreciation for his ignoring the official two-week camping limit in our case.

When we arrived in Santa Fe we knew no one. The first dozen people we met, it seemed, had no visible means of support. They drove school buses, sat art galleries for vacationing owners, things like that. One fellow sought to make ends meet by tie-dying T-shirts and baking herbal bread. When those efforts fell short, he advertised himself as a handyman in a classified ad, and frantically read how-to books at the library when called to do a job.

Our own way of getting by, before leaving Hyde Park, was first with jobs at the brand-new Santa Fe Downs racetrack, which now has closed. I was a bartender, Laurie sold sandwiches. When we tired of that, we played the horses out there, and for a little while actually made the $100 a week we needed to live. But then in one day we lost as much money as we had won the previous month. So I began freelancing, and Laurie became a waitress.

As we made friends, we invited them up to our tent, for cocktails and fancy dinners, cooked on the Coleman Stove. We got involved at the Community Theater, and soon were going to wild, eclectic parties, with half the guests wealthy, the other half barely getting by, and nobody caring one way or the other.

The town had only two indoor movie theaters, plus two drive-ins, all showing badly outdated films. Only four or five restaurants served liquor, but most others allowed diners to brown-bag their own wine, although it was technically illegal. The opening of the first McDonald's, out on Cerrillos Road, was such a big deal that Gov. Bruce King himself cut the ribbon.

The Plaza area was Santa Fe's commercial hub then, with drugstores, barbershops, clothing stores, Woolworth's, Sears, J.C. Penney and a Safeway. All the banks were home-owned. The closest thing to a mall was the strip of stores at Cordova Road and St. Francis Drive. The city's population was 45,000 people.

When Laurie and I realized we were going to stay, I hired on as a reporter at Santa Fe's daily paper, *The New*

Mexican. But it was asleep on its feet back then, and I was young and zealous. So I quit after a year, and Laurie and I began working to start a weekly, to be called the *Santa Fe Reporter*. All we could raise was $70,000, but it turned out to be enough. With only the tired daily, and four unambitious radio stations, the town was starved for news. The *Reporter* debuted in June 1974.

A blink of an eye ago. How much Santa Fe has changed since then. Life was gentler, cheaper, slower in the 1970s—and slower yet in the '40s, '50s and '60s before we came. Living here was easier in those days, before the skyrocketing real estate, the hilltop mansions, the tony shops, the "discovery" of Santa Fe, the big-box chain stores, the conglomerization of the world.

I doubt that a newcomer now could live the story I lived.

I look back upon those days with longing, and regret that they are gone. Yet when asked about it, I reply: "Yes, Santa Fe has changed, and not for the better—*but it's still the best place I know*." Change is constant everywhere, but I cannot name another small city with Santa Fe's blend of beauty, culture, tradition, open-mindedness, climate, and fiercely defended, unique identity.

And for three decades now, I have had the privilege of telling much of Santa Fe's story—and the wider story of the strange and fascinating state named New Mexico. My group sold the *Santa Fe Reporter* in 1988; but I keep writing about this place that I love.

As the world slips into the new millennium, Santa Fe's and New Mexico's best hope for the future rests in the past. Changes will keep coming, but each should be weighed, resisted, and only grudgingly accepted. We have something special here, special in all the world. Let's guard it for the next thousand years.

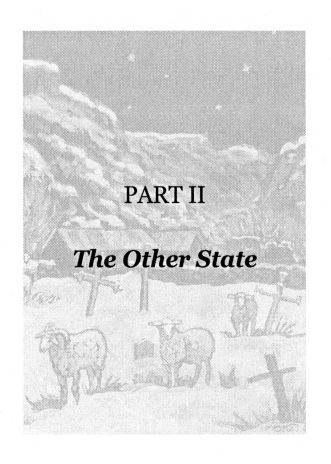

PART II

The Other State

The Squaw Man

*T*he year was 1960 or '61, at Christmastime. A
ferocious snowstorm was blowing into El Morro from the
west. The squaw man was sinking into a murderous rage.
The traveling salesman was thinking he had made a
mistake. And Ellen Bradbury, who tells the story, was a
young bride, barely out of her teens.

Today Bradbury heads Recursos, a Santa Fe
company that conducts tours into the area's remotest
regions. She grew up in New Mexico, and knows its ways.
But never before or since has she seen anything like that
fateful storm at El Morro. She was newly married, and her
husband was an archaeologist with the National Park
Service, stationed at El Morro National Monument in far
northwestern New Mexico, where Zuni and Navajo lands
come together. The couple lived in a government log cabin.

The nearby town of Ramah had just a handful of
residents. One of them was an Anglo "squaw man," who
had married a Navajo woman and with her ran the only
gas station and bar in town. The few other non-Indians in

Ramah were mostly Mormon. The squaw man was moody, hostile and probably an alcoholic. For some reason he refused to sell gas on Tuesdays, and when hapless travelers pulled up to his pump on that day, he chased them away at the point of the rifle he always kept handy. He was generally despised, and not just for his ornery ways. Both the Mormons and the Indians disapproved of liquor, and resented him for selling it. And because he was an Anglo with an Indian wife, he was not accepted into either culture.

As Christmas drew near in '60 or '61—Bradbury is now not sure which—grim black clouds foretold an imminent blizzard. But when the snowflakes began to swirl she was not worried, for like everyone out there, she had emergency provisions set aside. A few miles away, however, a lone salesman traveling in his car was growing alarmed. For diversion he had left Route 66 on his way to Gallup, unaware that the only road through El Morro country was unpaved. Now he feared being caught in the storm. When he saw a gas station up ahead, he sighed with relief.

But on that day, the squaw man had snapped. With his rifle he gunned down his wife. Then he stabbed her again and again with a screwdriver. Finally, standing at his gasoline pump, he shot himself in the head. As he fell, his arm became entangled in the hose, which held him upright. In death he seemed to awaiting the next customer.

The next customer was the salesman. With horror he saw that the man at the pump was dead. Then he saw the bleeding squaw, who had crawled outside and was still alive. Somehow he got her into his car and frantically went looking for help. The only other store in town was run by a

Mormon woman, who had closed up early in the now-furiously-falling snow. The salesman pounded on the door until she came, but she offered no help. She was leaving to see her children in a Christmas pageant in Ramah, where they would wait out the storm. And though Ramah was on the road to the hospital in Gallup, 55 miles away, she did not want to get her truck's upholstery stained with the Navajo woman's blood.

Not knowing what else to do, the salesman set out for Gallup himself, in the face of the blizzard. Miraculously he made it, but only by following a big logging truck all the way. Yet despite his heroic efforts, the woman died in the hospital.

The New Mexico State Police in Gallup sent out calls for someone to investigate the crime. But the Zuni police refused because it did not concern their people, and the Navajo police refused because they had to get supplies to Indians stranded in hogans in the storm. Finally Bradbury's husband was called, but the snow was too deep for his government Jeep to get through.

Three days later a snowplow reached the site. The squaw man, frozen solid, was still at his grisly post. Because the ground was also frozen, he could not be buried right away. So his body was laid out in an unheated shed behind the station for weeks, until the earth softened enough for graves to be blasted out for him and another fellow who died that winter.

Bradbury was only peripherally involved in this drama, which remains a legend in El Morro country. But of course she will never forget it. "It's really a 19th-century story," she says. "Life the way it used to be. But it happened in my life." And though she was amazed at the time, she now takes a tougher view of why no one but the out-of-town salesman was willing to get involved. "The squaw man was dead, his wife was dying. There was no help for either of them. People saw no reason to put themselves in peril. And there was no reason."

The Graveyard Fiesta

*A*s the July sun was setting, Bonny Christina Celine was alone in Calvary Cemetery in the Martineztown section of Albuquerque. Aside from her thoughts, the only thing she heard was the din of traffic from the nearby Big I, where Interstate 25 meets Interstate 40. She had come to tell a friend goodbye.

Dolores Gonzales was the receptionist in Celine's business office. A few days earlier Dolores had gone into surgery for the removal of what seemed to be a benign tumor. Something went terribly wrong, and she died in the operating room. She was just 32. Celine was inconsolable. She did not attend the burial, but a few hours later was sitting at the foot of her friend's grave. She planned to stay until the sun was gone.

In the deepening gold she remembered how much Dolores had loved to laugh. She recalled the joy Dolores brought to work each day, the pride she felt for her job and her young son, the big smile for everyone, the playful elbow in the ribs. Celine remembered that Dolores' favorite thing was dancing, into the wee hours. Dolores was the life of any party, and anywhere she went became a party. But now the party was over.

The death was a total shock. Nobody was ready for it. Dolores had worked the day before she went to the hospital, and everyone from the office was planning to visit her there as she recuperated. But Celine was away from work on that last day, and did not bid her friend farewell. Now she was trying to apologize. She could not tell if she was getting through. The only thing she felt in the stillness was a crushing grief. Then without warning the silence of the dead was broken.

Through the cemetery's entrance on Edith Boulevard came a procession of five automobiles. Two were stretch limousines, shiny gray and adorned with flowers and crépe-paper streamers. The cars drove slowly past Celine, and stopped at a headstone down the way. The doors popped open. Like a flock of doves, out flew a wedding party into the golden light.

The pretty teen-aged bride was in sequined white. Her proud new husband and his handsome Hispanic groomsmen were tuxedoed in black. The bridesmaids all wore cobalt blue, and the dress of someone's mother was shimmering pink. Moist with recent summer rains, the graveyard that enclosed them was as green as a garden.

They held hands in a circle around the grave. Sounds of laughter and happy Spanish singing floated through the tombstones of Calvary Cemetery. Prayers were said, and memories were called back to life. Every celebrant lifted a long-stemmed goblet, and each was filled to the brim with pink champagne.

From the little hill on which she stood, Celine could hear the clink of crystal. She felt thrilled, blessed, awed. Without moving or speaking she gazed down on the fiesta, while her thoughts drifted back over the festival occasions of her own life: lawn parties in New England, square dances on the Dakota prairie, powwows in the Indian Country of Oklahoma, hoedowns in southern New Mexico. Yes, she reminded herself, there is truly a time for every purpose under heaven.

The sky softened to pinks and violets, and still the celebration went on. Suddenly Celine felt an elbow poking her lightly in the ribs. Or maybe she only imagined it, as well as the voice that was saying: "They must have loved that person very much—but it's Saturday night, and now those young people should be going out to dance."

As though hearing the same voice, the wedding party jumped back into the rented limousines and the other cars. Again the procession filed past Celine. This time everybody waved gaily at her. In the last light of day, she waved back at them all, and smiled.

The Dead Ringer

*I*n the summer of 1989, 22-year-old Billy Cox of
Bartow, Florida, got a hankering to go west for the first
time, looking for adventure. He got off the Greyhound bus
in Roswell, New Mexico, and wandered into the local
museum. The historian there, Ken Hobbs, took one look,
gasped, and pronounced Cox a dead ringer for the most
famous outlaw ever to pass through those parts: Billy the
Kid. For Cox, it was the start of something ... well,
peculiar.

A few days later Ken Hobbs drove Billy Cox to the
nearby town of Lincoln, where the Kid killed several men
before he was gunned down 100 miles away in Fort
Sumner, New Mexico, in 1881 by Sheriff Pat Garrett, at the
age of 21. "This is Billy the Kid from Florida," Hobbs said
to his friend Jack Rigney, the ranger running the state
historical monument about those wild days in Lincoln.
Rigney could not believe his eyes.

Only one authenticated photograph of the Kid was
known to exist. In it he wears a crumpled hat, a low-slung

gunbelt and a bandanna, and holds a Winchester rifle at his side. The camera captures his face straight-on. The face in that photograph and Billy Cox's were identical.

After the ranger caught his breath, he and Cox struck a quick rapport. They stayed in touch after Billy took the bus back home a few days later and resumed his work as a busboy in a restaurant. Rigney visited relatives in Florida that winter and stopped by to see Billy, who had rounded up some clothes such as the Kid wore in the old tintype photo, and had been practicing the same pose.

As soon as Rigney saw Billy Cox intentionally impersonating Billy the Kid, he began seeing possibilities. So he suggested that Cox spend the next summer in Lincoln, to see what would happen. "Jack even said there could be a 'financial supplement' to this," Cox said later. "But I wasn't sure what he meant."

Billy returned to Lincoln in July 1990, and stayed in a room in Rigney's house. As he walked through town packing a Colt .45 pistol and a Winchester, both unloaded, tourists pointed at him in astonishment. Then they wanted him to pose for pictures, and paid him five or 10 dollars without him having to ask. When there was a crowd, he could pick up $30 or $40 at a time. At daily presentations at the state monument, Rigney would tell the story of Billy the Kid, then ask if anyone believed in ghosts. On cue, Cox would walk in and strike the pose. The tourists would gasp, grab for their cameras—and leave a donation.

In his spare time, Cox tried to do things that the first Billy had done in Lincoln County, more than 100 years ago. He borrowed horses and rode the open country. He slept out under the stars. He did odd jobs on area ranches, and accepted handouts at many of them. He went to saloons in the old village of White Oaks, where *señoritas* would dance with him and call him *"Billito"*— Little Billy. Yet Cox held onto his own identity, he insisted later. He never felt he was mystically bonded with the Kid, much less a reincarnation. "I was always William H. Cox, not William H. Bonney," he said. "There were never any spirits in the night."

In this fashion, the summer passed. Capitalizing on New Mexico's endless fascination with its most notorious son, Cox portrayed Billy not only in Lincoln but also at festivals in the southern towns of Truth or Consequences and Taiban, and at the Eastern State Fair in Roswell. He won look-alike contests, staged shootouts with "Pat Garrett's Gang," was featured on local television and in national magazines, even had a video made about him. The money was always chancy, but enough to keep him in canned pork and beans.

But the tourist season finally ended—and in October Cox realized that things were changing. Rigney, in whose house he had lived all summer, started dropping hints about Florida. Then the deputy sheriff of Lincoln County drove up one day and asked him outright: "When you going back home, Billy?" Some cattle on nearby ranches had been shot, it seemed, and people suspected him. "The deputy thought I was getting lost in the character," Cox explained. "He said he had seen it before."

Protesting his innocence, Cox nevertheless left town. Until the end of the year he stayed in the area, taking hospitality from friends in Roswell, Carrizozo and other places. Then he went home to Florida for two months. But the next March he returned to Lincoln. This time, however, he could not tell if he was really welcome.

Jack Rigney seemed glad to see him, and talked of reviving the Billy the Kid act in July and August. But there was no invitation to stay in Rigney's house in the meantime. And though the deputy sheriff was friendly at first, he soon returned to inquire about an apparent break-in at a Lincoln hotel, in a room once occupied by the Kid.

Not quite knowing what to make of all this, Cox "fled to Albuquerque" for several weeks, to figure out what to do. He really was wanting to go back to Lincoln in the summer and portray the Kid one more season before leaving the legendary gunfighter behind and getting on with his own life. Yet if the atmosphere did not seem right, he was ready with a backup plan. "If worse comes to worst," he said, "I'll go to Fort Sumner."

The Desert Trail

*I*n the blazing August sun in 1998, on a 600-foot-tall ledge in the magnificent canyon country of Utah, I was giving my 13-year-old niece from Atlanta her very first taste of the West. Though where we stood was hot and dry, we could see in the distance, maybe 100 miles south in the Four Corners region where New Mexico, Arizona, Utah and Colorado meet at one point, a huge dark storm.

I told my niece that as parched as the ground below us obviously was, I was glad we were not hiking down there on this day. Every year, I explained, people get killed by rain falling many miles away. Looking at the driest land she had ever seen, she found my report hard to believe.

The next day's news told of 10 unsuspecting hikers swept to their deaths by a flash flood in a narrow canyon in the Red Rock country of Arizona, killed by the same storm we had seen. When the water struck, they had been walking in the sun.

It all brought back my own first trip to the West, as a 24-year-old emerging from Georgia. I was hypnotized by the wide-open spaces, humbled by the towering mountains, seduced by the exotic Indian and Hispanic cultures. But not until Zion National Park in Utah did the danger hit home.

Before then I was seeing the West through my windshield—so much space to cover, so little time. But at Zion I finally parked at a trailhead to get out and hike. I took along a self-guiding leaflet. And that was the start of something big.

The text of the pamphlet told what would be seen on the hike. But the full back page was a scary list of warnings:

➼ STAY ON THE TRAIL. The desert has few landmarks, and it is easy to get disoriented or lost—which can result in death.

➼ CARRY PLENTY OF WATER. The combination of heat and low humidity rapidly dehydrates the body—which can result in death.

➼ SHIELD YOURSELF FROM THE SUN. In just a few minutes the sun can severely burn human skin—causing pain and even death.

➼ BEWARE OF RATTLESNAKES. They are plentiful in this area—and their poisonous bite can result in death.

➼ BEWARE OF SCORPIONS. Less deadly than rattlesnakes, the scorpion still must be avoided—for its bite too can be fatal.

➼ DO NOT THROW ROCKS. Portions of the trail below switchbacks are out of sight—and stones can cause injury or death to other hikers.

➻ STAY BACK OF CLIFF LEDGES. There are no guardrails, and falls from any height can result in serious injury—or death.

There were more, but the bottom line of every caution was the same: Any mess-up out in the real West can kill somebody.

I found this most exciting. As a child in a comfortably tamed part of the East, I thrilled to Western movies in which the sun or rattlesnakes or wolves or the endless desert posed disaster for the manly hero. If only I could live in such exciting country! Surely I would triumph over every threat.

But on that Utah desert trail, my boyhood fantasies took on a frightening overcast. The dangers that had seemed distant and romantic were suddenly real and present, with the actual power to kill people—like me. This was no longer the movies.

I realized at once that I liked the reality better than the celluloid image. The sun was as hot as it ever was in the Old West, the snakes as potent, nature just as unforgiving. If I fell or got lost or bitten, it wouldn't make much difference that modern, sophisticated help was just a few miles away. I could be as dead as anyone whose luck ran out 100 years ago.

I survived that hike without incident, but never forgot its lesson. Years later, when I moved to New Mexico, I did not mind when a cloudburst ripped open Hyde Park Road, stranding me in a tent in a campground for three days. I enjoyed the times when raging water made the arroyo to my Tesuque house impassable, leaving me stuck on whichever side I was on. I have loved the big snowstorms that occasionally paralyze Santa Fe. I'm sorry I barely missed the 40-below-zero freeze of 1971.

The theme to all these dramatic phenomena is that when all is said and done, nature is still bigger than man. This is ultimately true in big cities as well, but it is more visible out where we live. I feel sadness and horror when hikers get washed away, or when an old couple freezes to death looking for their dog on a mountain trail in the snow, just 200 yards from their automobile. But at bottom I love nature's majesty more.

The Apostrophe

*L*eaving, for the umpteenth time, my regular Tuesday-morning racquetball clash with my friend Chuck Poitras, I noticed for the very first time a most distressing fact: There is a typographical error in the sign that identifies Santa Fe's premier sports and recreational facility. "FT. MARCY/MAGER'S COMPLEX" the handsome wood-carved sign proclaims. But in truth it should say "MAGERS."

Ah, the wayward apostrophe, bane of language purists. Back when I was training copy editors at the *Santa Fe Reporter*, I had for them a standard rule concerning this troublesome little punctuation mark: "Whenever an apostrophe appears, it is wrong." (I also liked to cite the definition advanced by syndicated humor columnist Dave Barry: "The apostrophe is an indication to the reader that an 's' is coming up.")

Why the proper usage of this particular mark, among all the others, is so hard to grasp is puzzling. Like the comma, the period and the exclamation point, the apostrophe has its rules. But for some reason the rules elude most sign-makers. You see it every day on mailbox name plates: "The Jone's," "The Smith's," "The Ortega's," "The Martinez'"—not one of the apostrophes used correctly. When I was a schoolboy in Georgia, working at Jack Matthews' corner grocery, I remember how proud he was of his nifty new neon sign that beamed out "Matthew's Market"—until I pointed out that it meant "the market that belongs to Matthew."

But back to the subject at hand: the "FT. MARCY/MAGER'S COMPLEX," and the man whose name is meant to be honored there. Although probably just a few of the facility's users, native Santa Feans and newcomers alike, know or think about it, there was a man named Magers who left his mark on this site. His first name was Brady, and he was a football coach.

From 1927 to 1939 Brady Magers directed the team at Santa Fe High School. He was hired sight-unseen while completing his studies at the University of Kansas, and arrived to take over a dispirited program that regularly got stomped by the teams from Roswell and Clovis—and sometimes even by the Santa Fe Indian School. In those days football was not played below the high school level, so every year Magers had to instruct a new crop of freshmen in the basic intricacies of putting on their uniforms. Yet out of this rawest of raw material he shaped at least one player who went on to become a college All-American, at West Point. And he won Santa Fe's first-ever state championship.

The year was 1935, and the squad that year had exceptional talent. Yet it also was cocky and undisciplined. After a miserable showing against the Indian School,

Magers told his players he was so disgusted with them that he was quitting. When Monday practice came, the coach refused to take part. Chastened, the players, on their own, drilled harder than ever before on blocking, tackling and other basics. They begged Magers to return—and after he did, the team never lost again that year.

The state title game was played on Thanksgiving, in Santa Fe. The night before, three inches of snow fell. With no traction for either team, a glum scoreless tie seemed to be in the offing. But one Santa Fe player's father was warden of the state penitentiary; and by kickoff time a crew of prisoners had manually cleared the field. The Demons scored once and won.

Santa Fe's football field in those days was little more than a glorified pasture, with some bleachers for spectators. Magers felt his champions deserved more, so he made it happen. Like the rest of the country, this city was struggling through the Great Depression and was broke. But somehow Magers got the surveying, the grading, the plumbing, the construction, the grass and everything else donated for an imposing rock-walled stadium, the finest in the state of New Mexico. When it debuted in 1938, the players voted to give it his name.

Magers Field stood until the early 1980s, when it came down to make way for the new sports complex, which opened in 1984. About that same time, as I recall, Brady Magers—still a resident of Santa Fe—died, up around the age of 90. Today his memory has faded, and even his name is desecrated by an offending apostrophe. Somebody should take a wood chisel and chip the apostrophe right out of that sign. For the legacy of this notable Santa Fean, that would be the kindest cut of all.

The Ordinary House

No one knows just when it was built, although historical researcher Corinne Sze is trying to find out. No one famous is known to have lived there. It has just five rooms, plus two tiny bathrooms. But for the Historic Santa Fe Foundation, the purchase of the thick-adobe-walled Garcia House at 524 Alto Street was cause for celebration.

And indeed it *was* celebrated, at a gala party in in September 2000 in the *placita* of the adjacent Donaciano Vigil House. Because of limited space, only members of the Historic Foundation attended the event. But anyone who treasures the uniqueness of Santa Fe could also applaud this acquisition.

The Garcia House, which looks out upon the Santa Fe River just west of De Fouri Street downtown, is part of the Barrio de Guadalupe, named for the nearby Catholic church. Strictly speaking, the structure is not a free-standing house at all, but just one side of the sprawling Vigil House. Its five modest rooms are aligned in a linear strip, running north and south.

In a quick first assessment, the average Santa Fean—much less an outsider—might not grasp why the Garcia property was the subject of an urgent fund-raising letter from Historic Foundation chairman Peter Wirth, or why the foundation paid some $200,000 for it. At first glance, the house seems extremely ordinary.

But according to the foundation's executive director, Lois Snyderman, it is the ordinariness itself that makes the Garcia House a vital part of Santa Fe's heritage. "There's a term called 'vernacular architecture,'" she explains. "It means just the way things were. An individual building may not have any particular importance, but we feel it's terribly important to preserve the look of a neighborhood—and of the past."

Whatever the historical details may be, the house was part of a past very different from the present in central Santa Fe. Well into the 20th century, the Barrio de Guadalupe remained a neighborhood of cultivated fields watered by *acequias* tapping into the river. Such agricultural compounds have now almost disappeared from the scene.

But at this site on Alto Street, striking remnants of the past remain. In the late 1950s sculptor Boris Gilbertson and his companion Charlotte White bought the rambling, adjacent Vigil property, then for the next 20 years renovated it in a way that was artistically stunning yet historically sensitive.

Gilbertson died in 1982; White lives on and continues to occupy the Vigil House. But four years ago she donated her entire huge complex to the Historic Foundation, stipulating only that she be allowed to reside there during her lifetime. For this notable act of generosity, White was named a Santa Fe Living Treasure in 2000.

White remembers boarded-up windows from the Garcia House opening onto the *placita* of her property when she and Gilbertson first moved in. She suspects—but has no evidence—that the structure was part of the original compound, which perhaps dates back to the late 1700s. So when owner Mariano Garcia put the house up for sale early in 2000, the foundation jumped for it.

Historical researcher Sze emphasizes that tracing the lineage of the house will be difficult. "But there's no doubt that it's old." Ancient property records are hazy, she says, but modern ones indicate that the little house was sold in 1927 to one Piedad Silva, and then was bought 20 years later, in 1947, by Mariano Garcia—for $600.

Until mid-2000 Garcia and a brother, Patricio, lived within the house's three-foot-thick adobe walls. They did little to modernize the old place—which suits its new owner just fine. Although the foundation does plan to renovate the house and then, for income, rent it out as a residence, its style will meticulously be preserved.

"We are very, very pleased that we were able to raise the money to buy the house," sums up executive director Snyderman. "It was a cliff-hanger there for a while, because other people were definitely interested in the property. But we got it.

"The Garcia brothers were just ordinary people doing ordinary things. We really value that aspect. So many ordinary houses in Santa Fe have been renovated out of existence."

The Maestro

Adelina Timofeyew has led a life of music. The choice was a personal one, and she has achieved considerable distinction through her talent, hard work and devotion. Things might have been easier if she had tried to use the family connection . . . but we'll get to that a little later. The point is, she did it her way.

She was born and raised in Albuquerque, in a large Italian-American clan that proudly traces its origins to the city of Lucca in the Tuscany region of the old country. For three generations her family has been prominent in New Mexico. Her grandparents built the grand old Kimo Theater and other landmarks in Albuquerque. U.S. Sen. Pete Domenici also comes from this Italian colony.

"Ever since I was born," Adelina Timofeyew says, "I have wanted to study music." So shortly after World War II she went as a young woman to Rome, Italy, to learn it all—voice, piano, composition, dance—from the world's finest teachers. While there she met another young musician, Nicolay Timofeyew, who became her husband.

He was a world-class tenor, but "he was born under an ugly star." He was Russian by birth but grew up in Yugoslavia, and when he refused to do military service for the post-war Communist government there, he became a man without a country.

Because of his lack of citizenship he could not perform in Europe or the United States in those years. So he and his wife spent the early 1950s touring South America "inch by inch," from one seedy concert hall to another. A little girl was born to them in that time, and they hauled her along on the dreary road. "It seemed that one country after another was having a revolution," Adelina says. "It was a miserable time to be there."

Because of his marriage to an American, Timofeyew eventually was allowed to enter this county. He went straight to New York, and when talent agencies there heard his magnificent voice he was signed immediately. But then his health broke. To provide an education and a family environment for their daughter, the Timofeyews returned to her home in Albuquerque. There Adelina took care of her husband until his death in 1982. She also resumed her own musical interests, slowly at first, giving voice and piano lessons.

Adelina Timofeyew went on to become president of the New Mexico Women Composers Guild, a surprisingly distinguished organization, considering the small population of this state. Almost every year it wins national awards, and each winter a formal concert of its works is presented in Albuquerque. Adelina's own compositions have often been honored. Her "Indian Suite" for woodwind quintet was the centerpiece of one of the winter concerts. The National Federation of Music Clubs featured her work one year, and two compositions were presented in Boston in 1981. She also gives private concerts and continues to teach.

Thus Adelina Timofeyew worked past the tragedy of her husband's life and career to earn acclaim on her own. She never turned away from the musical star that led her as a child, and today she is a widely recognized composer. And she did it without the family connection, which she is reluctant even to mention.

For her name before she married was Adelina Puccini—and yes, her family is indeed related to the legendary Italian composer Giacomo Puccini, whose magnificent operas include "La Boheme," "Tosca" and "Madama Butterfly." The relationship is a distant one, "not in a direct line," although The Maestro, as she calls him, did also come from Lucca in Tuscany. Her own family, she recalls, never made much of their famous great-granduncle, or whatever he was.

She dimly remembers a story about The Maestro passing through Albuquerque by train while researching his 1910 opera "Girl of the Golden West." He had a few hours' layover, and he visited a poor piano teacher named diMauro, a friend from student days, who had become part of New Mexico's Italian colony. But she does not know the details.

In fact, her family's only direct contact with The Maestro was apparently not a pleasant one. Her father, Luigi Puccini, was a journalist for an Italian-American newspaper in New York before he settled down in Albuquerque. He was a great admirer of his famous but distant relative, and once tried to approach The Maestro in New York. "But my father came back very insulted."

Again she does not know the details. "My parents never spoke very much about their lives. I'm not sure what happened. The Maestro was very strange about relatives and people who claimed to be relatives. He didn't want them around. Whatever it was, my father was very insulted about something. After that, he never spoke about The Maestro."

That painful event took place before she was born, but it left an impression upon her life. "My father always told me to stand on my own feet," she says. "When I told him I wanted to be a musician he told me to stand on my own feet, and not on anyone else's laurels." Which is what Adelina Timofeyew has done.

The Compound Caper

*T*he Compound restaurant on Canyon Road was beyond question THE place to dine when I arrived in Santa Fe in the early 1970s. The city had few places with any semblance of elegance then, and archaic and politically rigged liquor laws allowed just a handful to serve wine or cocktails. But the Compound had it all.

With tuxedoed and white-gloved waiters, a superb Continental menu and an enforced requirement that gentlemen wear coats and ties and ladies be comparably attired, the Compound set a tone not found anywhere else. Everyone knew it was the top of the line. It was pricey, but you got your money's worth.

The cost kept me from being a regular, but when I did go, I never knew who might be there. One time it was film actor Joel Grey, fresh from his Academy Award for "Cabaret." Another time it was actress Angela Lansbury, at the height of her "Murder, She Wrote" TV-series fame. One Christmas I splurged, and partook of the Compound's celebrated nine-course holiday feast—each course accented by its own special wine.

In the mid-1970s the Compound was bought outright by its dapper and impeccable manager, Victor Sagheer. Of Lebanese lineage, Sagheer had an Old World style and charm that had made the restaurant the paragon that it was. Now instead of creating a masterpiece for other owners, he would do it for himself.

I was editor of the young *Santa Fe Reporter* at that time, and we wrote a duly respectful business story about the sale. But we also had a weekly guest column called "Open Door"—and on that particular week, the expected article was not delivered. We flew pretty much by the seat of our pants back then, and as our final deadline loomed, I searched frantically in my files for a substitute story to fill the space. Nothing! It was the basic journalistic nightmare. I had to produce something, and fast.

Then inspiration born of desperation struck. *The Compound!* Yes, that was it! People were talking about the sale, the place was a local landmark, reader interest would be high. But rather than just reheating the business story, I slipped into an antic mode. Figuring that the Compound was so firmly entrenched as the *crème de la crème* of Santa Fe restaurants that its repute was impregnable, I decided to poke a little fun at it.

Under a *nom de plume* meant to underline the gag, I batted out a totally facetious story about some changes the new owner had in mind. Careful to refer neither to the Compound nor Victor Sagheer by name, to make it obvious that the column was a spoof, I let myself have a good old time. According to the story, a "well-known east-side dining establishment" was about to undergo a complete change of identity under its "ambitious new master."

Supposedly the new proprietor planned to make his restaurant far less formal, in keeping with Santa Fe's casual ways. Accordingly, he planned to change the cuisine from Continental to Mexican. To entertain guests as they waited to be seated, he was going to install pool tables in the lobby; and to amuse them as they dined, he would also add a jukebox. An overdue modernization would be a drive-up window for people too busy to come inside. And the name would be changed to "Vic's Place."

Chuckling all the way, I got that story out and into print in time to meet the deadline. Then upon rereading it in the paper the next day, I felt it was so nonsensical as to be truly funny. But Mr. Sagheer, I'm afraid I must say, was NOT amused.

Through an employee at the Compound, I was told that he was confounded and offended by the article, and was thinking about suing the *Reporter*. Surprised, I called him to try to explain—and if need be, apologize for—"Vic's Place." He was somewhat mollified, but did not laugh. The gap between a young writer's brash humor and Mr. Sagheer's ingrained elegance was simply too great. So the episode went down (dare I say this?) with a bad taste for us both.

Now Victor Sagheer has himself sold the Compound, after running it as manager and owner for 33 years. I hope somewhere along the way he forgave the *Reporter* for its long-ago gag. And I hope the new owners can uphold his golden standard of excellence.

The Hermitage

In the foothills of the mountains just east of Santa Fe, really quite close to the heart of town, someone has built a home with his own hands. It is a modest dwelling, with just one room. It has no plumbing, no telephone, no electricity, and only a crude fireplace for heat and cooking. It provides only the barest protection from wind, rain, cold and snow.

The house is a shanty, which I found by accident one day while hiking with my dog, Max. Tired of the familiar trail into the hills, I left it to make my own way up to the top of a knob, to check out the view. Two-thirds of the way up, I clambered over some big rocks—and there, a dozen yards in front of me, was the house.

Its setting was well-thought-out, ingenious, camouflaged. A great outcropping of rock shielded it from the view of anyone on the trail up a higher hill to the east. Piñons and junipers hid it on the other sides. The surrounding terrain was steep, rugged, raw.

Ten weathered 20-foot poles, which looked like they might have come from a tepee, formed a simple A-frame, more horizontal than vertical. Green canvas, formerly a tent, was draped roughly over it. Odd pieces of lumber—two-by-fours, two-by-eights, one-by-sixes, remnants of crates—provided structure on the sides where the boulders did not. A four-foot square of Plexiglas made a window. Flaps of fabric and leather, whipping in the spring wind, were the walls and the entrance.

As my astonishment subsided, curiosity took its place. Cautiously I approached. If the house was abandoned, I wanted to examine it. If occupied, I wanted to pass a friendly word with whoever lived there. I hoped I would not get shot. Suddenly three furiously barking dogs, two brown and one black, were upon me. Without even a stick to fend them off, I figured to get chewed up a little for sure. But they were not very big, and after sounding their alarm seemed friendly enough, and backed off. Despite the ruckus, there was no activity in the house. I called out a greeting, but nobody was home.

So I went up for a look. Large gaps in construction left the little shelter open to the sun and air; and though I did not enter, everything inside was visible. A red Confederate flag was hanging from a pole. Makeshift wooden shelves held several old coffee cans with snap-top lids sealing the current contents against the weather. There were a dozen or more books, but except for two Bibles and one named "Transcend," I could not make out their titles.

Very little food was evident. Several plastic water jugs were strung from a rope. Two packages of tortillas and a big box of powdered milk, labeled in Spanish, were on a shelf. Some fire-blackened metal utensils rested upon a simple grill that had been built from stacked rocks, some of which must have weighed 200 pounds or more.

Art supplies—brushes, paints, an easel—were here and there, and a pretty good sketch of one of the dogs stood on a little table about 15 inches tall, next to a post card of the Apache chief Geronimo. Also on the table was a coffee mug marked "United Blood Services." A cheap plastic mask of a skull lay about, and along one wall was a set of skis.

In the most protected corner, up against the rock, was a metal cot, and atop it a foam mattress and a sleeping bag. On coat hangers above were a few men's clothes—shirts and pants—all well-worn. Neither the cot nor the clothing, nor anything else in the house, was well shielded from the elements. Blowing rain would get everything wet.

Outside, a black rubber bag with a two-foot hose hung from a big juniper. "Solar-Powered Shower" was printed on its side. A sheet of plywood was leaning against another tree, to create a doghouse. In several places the abundant rocks had been lined up and stacked in rows, as though to landscape the grounds.

The place was quite a production. I waited a little while, but its resident did not return. Then I had to be on my way. Now I keep wondering what sort of man built this house. Is he a hermit, an anti-social recluse? Is he a homeless person who would rather sleep in the hills than under a bridge? Is he an unreconstructed hippie, still living off the land decades after the movement has passed? Is he young or old, employed or jobless, a student, a mystic? Does he live there by choice or necessity?

From his high hillside he can look down upon numerous $400,000 houses under construction below, many of them "second homes" for moneyed outsiders who will leave them empty most of the year. I wonder how he feels about these houses.

I've thought a lot about this man I've never met. I think I admire him. I like his toughness, ingenuity and enterprise. I appreciate the physical strength and patience that he put into his home. I hope his dogs and his varied interests help fill the solitude. It seems to me that his humble dwelling harms no one. And I am impressed by his novel solution to Santa Fe's high cost of housing.

The Code Talkers

A dignitary from the Northern Mariana Islands in the South Pacific went recently to the Four Corners region to pay homage to the Navajo Code Talkers, who played a key role in freeing his homeland from the Japanese in World War II. If the Mariana Islands still honor the Code Talkers after more than half a century, so should we.

When America went to war in the Pacific after the attack on Pearl Harbor in 1941, the country desperately needed military codes that the ready-and-waiting Japanese could not crack. The success of the war effort largely hinged upon it. A civil engineer in Los Angeles, who as a boy had spent time in Navajoland with his missionary parents, remembered the mystifyingly complex language spoken by the people there. He suggested to the Marines that a code might be based on Navajo.

A call for 30 volunteers went to the reservation. The volunteers—some of whom were too old or too young for Marine duty, but lied about their age—did not know what the mission would be when they answered the call in

1942. Once they learned, they were sworn to absolute secrecy, upon pain of execution.

The Choctaw Indian dialect had been a code in World War I, baffling the Germans who intercepted it on telephone lines. But the Japanese knew this, and fully expected American Indian languages to be used against them. Thus to avoid having their messages deciphered, the Navajos could not merely send messages in their tongue, but had to devise a code for it as well.

By the summer of 1942 the volunteers were ready with a 450-word code. Then 300 more Navajos were recruited to memorize it. In August of that year, their "secret weapon" got its baptism of fire in the bloody battle of Guadalcanal. It withstood that test—and all the others that followed. The Navajo code proved as vital for its speed as for its impenetrability. Messages could be encoded, transmitted and decoded in 20 seconds by the Navajos. Sophisticated military cryptography machines needed half an hour for the job.

Soon the Japanese realized that complicated instructions for precise military operations were being transmitted in a maddening new code. Though they could pick up and listen to the broadcasts, the information being sent remained a secret.

Working furiously, the Japanese began to close in on the code. When they determined that it used an American tribal language, they subjected Indian prisoners of war to brutal interrogations. Identifying it as Navajo, they tortured a Navajo captured in the Bataan Death March to tell them what was being said. But though he could recognize words, he could not make out the message, and thus could provide no useful information.

As the war proceeded with no compromise of the code, the Marines designated it for their most sensitive operations. American units mistakenly bombarded with "friendly fire" needed this code to call off errant artillery—otherwise, the plea for relief might be coming from an enemy fluent in English. For the colossal assault upon Iwo Jima, a make-or-break beachhead for the planned invasion of Japan, the Navajo code was the only one considered secure enough to use. The code also helped win the battles of Tinian, Saipan, the Marianas, Tarawa and countless others, remembered and forgotten.

As long as World War II raged on, the stymied Japanese never broke the Navajo code—the only one they failed to crack. But after the war was over, the monumental service rendered by the Code Talkers went unheralded until 1968. Only then did futuristic computers move beyond the Navajo code, allowing its formerly "top-secret" role to be unveiled.

Time has taken its toll on the Code Talkers. Now just an ever-dwindling few remain alive, but still they gather to commemorate with fierce pride the unique contribution they made toward saving their country, as well as many others. And every now and then, an emissary journeys all the way from some place like the Northern Mariana Islands, 1,300 miles south of Tokyo in the vast Pacific Ocean, out to the red rocks of Navajoland, just to say: Thank you. Well done.

The Lady Jocks

*I*n the passing parade of things, this one was not the biggest. The girls basketball team from St. Michael's High School in Santa Fe beat the girls from West Las Vegas High School, 60 miles down the road, in the District 2AAA tournament. Or as the headline said, the Lady Horsemen beat the Lady Dons.

Both teams brought losing records into the post-season elimination, and one of them had to lose the match. Nor could the winner expect to advance much further. What intrigued me was something outside the action. What was fascinating was the very concept: that "Lady Horsemen" and "Lady Dons" could even exist, much less do combat with each other. It defied the tenets of two proud languages, and also the laws of biology. It was a hoot.

But I wonder if anyone else saw it that way.

The naming of sports teams is often an irrational business, in which fierce emotions leave clear thought and discourse behind. Then once a name is chosen, it becomes "tradition." Take the "Lady Horsemen." Undoubtedly the name's origin goes back to the time when only boys played sports for St. Michael's. They took the Horseman as their symbol—and it was a good one, blending romance and both the Western and Spanish heritages. By the time changing mores dictated that girls should have teams too, the Horsemen had a proud tradition—and the girls got stuck with it. The same thing happened to the Lady Dons, who play under a Spanish title of respect for men. When naming time came, in both cases it was a no-brainer. Literally.

So here we have female men on horses clashing with female gentlemen, and nobody giving it a second thought. Still, it could be worse. What if we had the Women Horsemen vs. the Women Dons? Ah, but so too could it be better. I think the answer for both teams, if anyone cares, could come from the gracefulness of the Spanish language.

Yes, the English word "Horsewomen" is clunky, which probably is why it was rejected in the first place. But how about *Caballeras*? Now there's a pretty word, and plausible as well. It means a woman on horseback. St. Mike's, it seems to me, should be proud to be symbolized on fields of athletic valor by the Horsemen AND the *Caballeras*. The names are synonymous, are linguistically and anatomically correct, and both honor the Western/ Spanish heritage. And the combination would be out-of-the-ordinary, another plus.

Over in West Las Vegas, the answer is not quite as simple. The easy fix, of course, would be to name the girls team the *Doñas*—the female counterpart to the *Dons*. But in the English-speaking society, most people would not get it. Soon the school's teams would be known as the Dons and the Donnas, bringing chuckles and lack of understanding.

But what if the girls were the *Duquesas*? Now there's a noble pairing: a *don* and a *duquesa*—a duchess. Again, the terms are consistent, linguistically and anatomically plausible, and mindful of a proud heritage. The Spanish word *Duquesa* (or *Marquesa* or whatever) would soon become as familiar for West Las Vegas teams as the Spanish word *Lobo* (wolf) easily became for the University of New Mexico.

So that is my modest proposal. However, I do not expect it to go far. As noted, the name of an athletic team is an irrational affair, swayed far more by sentimentality, emotion and "tradition" than by due deliberation. What else could explain the Los Angeles Dodgers, in a town where—unlike the old Brooklyn—I don't think they YET have any trolleys to dodge? What else could deposit the Utah Jazz in Salt Lake City, where there is precious little jazz, most certainly no Bourbon Street —and hardly any bourbon? What else makes teams cling tenaciously to outdated and questionable names like the Cleveland Indians and the Atlanta Braves—and the obviously objectionable Washington Redskins?

Many colleges and high schools have dropped such symbols in recent years, and already their new names are settling in. And so would new names quickly become accepted for the Lady Horsemen and the Lady Dons. But I'm not holding my breath. Several years ago at a great center of learning and athletics, Colorado State University, the students were asked in a referendum if the time had come to rename the female teams. The result was a resounding vote to hold onto their traditional name: the Lady Rams.

The False Book

*R*ummaging through my bookshelf, I came across a slim volume that a while back touched off one of the most peculiar brouhahas in the history of publishing. At the very least it was surely the only book ever to make *The New York Times* best-seller list for both fiction *and* non-fiction. Beyond that, however, it also provided rare glimpses into the complexity of the human soul.

For the first 15 years of its existence, "The Education of Little Tree," a lovely childhood memoir, was accepted as the factual autobiography of an Oklahoma-born Cherokee orphan raised by his grandparents in the Tennessee mountains during the Great Depression. When first published in 1976, "Little Tree" did not sell well. It went out of print for 10 years. Then in 1986 the University of New Mexico Press bought rights to it for $500 and came out with a new edition—which quickly became a phenomenon.

Over the next five years it sold nearly 800,000 copies. It rose to No. 1 on the *Times* non-fiction list. The

American Booksellers Association voted it the book they most enjoyed recommending. Without heavy promotion, it developed a huge cult. I happily joined that cult, and gave copies to several friends.

But halfway through 1991 came a less happy discovery: that *Little Tree*'s author, listed as Forrest Carter, was in reality one Asa "Ace" Carter, a gun-toting, vicious Southern racist during the civil-rights struggles of the 1960s. Asa Carter's exploits included writing Alabama governor George Wallace's infamous "segregation forever" speech in 1963 as well as forming a paramilitary unit called the Original Ku Klux Klan of the Confederacy. He once was arrested after a Klan shooting, but the charges against him were later dropped.

This secret identity of "Forrest Carter," who died in 1979, was affirmed by both his brother and a literary scholar, who said that Carter used the alias to hide his racist background. It was a revelation that dismayed me, and thousands of others. How could such beauty come from such a vile mind? If there was no Indian child named Little Tree, if the events depicted in the book never took place, then was its whole message of tolerance and love now discredited? Was the gentle wisdom tucked into its pages now fit only for dupes?

And what of the decision by UNM Press to continue publishing *Little Tree* after the hoax was revealed? Was it nothing more than a cynical refusal to turn loose of its biggest moneymaker? Indeed, the scandal touched off a new surge in sales, with the book now listed as fiction not fact on *The New York Times* list.

Running across my copy of *Little Tree*, I pondered once again the questions it raised. I came up with the same answers I did back when the scandal broke. Whatever its origins, I concluded, the book was a work of remarkable beauty, of significant value to the world. Readers could still learn from its message of gentleness, tolerance and love, and UNM Press should keep on selling it.

Maybe late in life Asa Carter underwent a transformation, and wrote *Little Tree* as atonement for his racist days. Or maybe he did not change at all, but wrote the book out of some other part of his personality. If so, he would be a fascinating mixture of both good and evil—like most of the rest of us.

Still at play on the stage of the modern South is the eternal struggle between the forces of good and evil. And as with Asa Carter, I suspect that the most intense battles are still taking place within individual persons.

Cowardly arsonists, whose hate-fed urges have been held in check by societal pressures and perhaps their own consciences, are suddenly crossing over again to the dark side, putting the torch to black churches, burning them to the ground. And horrified white Southerners, whose parents smugly accepted racism as the proper way of life, have been stirred to look into their own hearts, and have rallied to aid the stricken blacks.

Asa/Forrest Carter was not the first man to fight his greatest fight within the confines of his own soul. Nor was he the last.

The Little World

A small piece of New Mexico history, a larger piece of Santa Fe history, and an enormous piece of my personal history passed from the scene on Thursday, June 12, 1997, when the ashes of Mabel Sanchez Hoefer were laid to rest in Fairview Cemetery.

For almost 20 years, from 1974 until 1993, Mabel was my landlady, in a rundown adobe compound on Galisteo Street in the South Capitol area. When I moved in, just before launching the *Santa Fe Reporter*, I needed something quick and cheap. Also I needed a place that would take a dog.

At first Mabel turned down the dog. No way, she said, she had strict rules against them. But I pleaded, and quickly she relented. Nothing about Mabel was really strict. And the price was definitely right: $175 a month, utilities included, for a five-room adobe with vigas, two fireplaces, an enclosed, shady patio and covered, off-street parking, seven blocks from the Plaza. Lease unnecessary— but she took a $35 damage deposit.

There were eight or nine units in her little domain, which in the 1960s she and her late husband, Herman, had run as a motel. Now a residential complex, the Galisteo Street enclave was her income—and the primary preoccupation of her life.

From her own quarters in the largest apartment, Mabel watched over things. Her main property-management principle was benign neglect—as in: "I won't ask for much in the way of rent if you won't ask for much in the way of service." This led to years between paint jobs, persistent leaks in the roof, long days with frozen pipes, and other inconveniences. But I was working 70-hour weeks in those early years, and was barely home long enough to notice, or care. Her way also gave me a fine appreciation of why New Mexico is called the "Land of Mañana"— everything eventually got taken care of, and life went on.

Delivering the monthly rent check to Mabel, I often stopped to chat. She almost always was home, as she did not drive and had health problems for as long as I recall. But she loved to talk, especially about her tenants and her relatives. That's when I learned her family's proudest claim to fame: that her grandmother's sister, in southern New Mexico, had had a baby with Billy the Kid. But the child was by now lost in history.

Anyway, Mabel was much more interested in the current history unfolding every day in her little corner of the world. Her low-rent apartments, some with only one or two rooms, drew a steady stream of occupants short on funds or luck or both.

Her most famous tenant during my long residency was the zany artist and notorious Santa Fe character Tommy Macaione, who moved next-door into a one-room unit after the city shut down his west-side house where he had kept dozens of stray dogs and cats in semi-wild conditions. But many of the other neighbors stand out just as clearly in my memory.

There was the sweet teen-age girl who came to have her baby. There was the World War II vet dying of emphysema, who seldom left his single room. The young painter who liked to travel to Nepal. The retired accountant and his frail wife, who never got over a brutal assault downtown one night. Some nice young couples, who stayed briefly while looking for larger places. The fierce woman who kept a huge Doberman pinscher named Hitler caged in her tiny yard, and got arrested for burning her infant child with a cigarette. A number of drunks, a number of "New-Agers." And a few people who later rose to prominent positions, here and elsewhere.

In time I could afford to move, but chose not to. I liked the flow of life through that place, and I liked Mabel. And I still couldn't beat the rent, which never topped $450, with utilities still included. Twice I raised the rent myself, when she just forgot about it for too long.

In 1993, however, Mabel was failing rapidly, and I knew my good thing could not last forever. So I bought, from her son Gilbert, a nearby house that she once had owned. "Good," she said. "It's staying in the family." When I moved away from Galisteo Street, she told me I had been her longest tenant ever.

But in June 1997, after a long illness, Mabel died at 77. With her died another part of a more innocent, more easygoing and better Santa Fe, in which many things were more important than money. I was fortunate that her history and mine were entwined along the way.

70

The Wolves

*T*he hoopla accompanying the long-awaited return of a few wild wolves to Yellowstone National Park has diverted attention, temporarily, from plans to establish a colony of wolves here in New Mexico. If things go as planned by the U.S. Fish and Wildlife Service, breeding pairs of Mexican gray wolves would be released in the Apache and Gila national forests down south as soon as the environmental impact has been fully assessed and the captive population of these near-extinct wolves reaches 100 to 150, a figure rapidly being approached.

Environmentalists, supported by a growing majority of the public, consider the wolf a normal part of the ecosystem, neither more nor less destructive than other creatures woven into nature's tapestry. And like any creature, they say, the wolf has a right to exist. But some people violently disagree.

Leading the anti-wolf charge is the ranching industry, in whose name wolves were virtually exterminated in the western United States in the late

1800s and early 1900s. The New Mexico Cattle Growers Association is dead-set against the program, invoking awful, bloody images of what it will bring: peril to the jobs, the pets, even the families of ranchers. "My grandpappy rid the range of those varmints," seems to be the mindset, "and I'll be GAWD-damned if I'll let 'em back!"

Thus in Silver City, New Mexico, cattle-growing interests have barraged radio listeners with lunatic advertisements that claim, among other things, that animal-rights activists have "a lot in common with Adolph Hitler's Nazis," that environmentalism is "rooted in pagan nature worship," and that the environmental movement's real agenda is to destroy first civilization and then the human race.

Those behind such claptrap, so filled with hate and lies, have made up their minds, and do not wish to be confused with facts. And that is unfortunate, especially where wolves are concerned. For the facts are both fascinating and surprising.

Over the past several years, relevant facts about wolves in the wild have meticulously been collected, not by some radical fringe but by the Fish and Wildlife Service itself. The data was required for the reintroduction program in Yellowstone.

Unlike this country, Canada did not eradicate its wolf population decades ago. When public attitudes began to change in recent times, wolves crossing over from Canada were allowed to remain in Montana and, especially, in Minnesota, where some 2,000 now are established. The federal study gathered statistics from these places, as well as a great deal of other information on wolves. The findings included:

➤ As long as records have been kept, there has never been a verified incident of a human in North America being killed or even seriously injured by a wild wolf—although many human deaths were caused by bears, cougars, bison, elk and other animals.

➤ From 1982 to 1993 in Montana, just three dogs are known to have been attacked by wolves, and only one of them died. In Minnesota, where 68,000 households are in the wolf range, fewer than five attacks on domestic dogs per year have been noted.

➤ Of 232,000 cattle in Minnesota's wolf range, only 55 were lost to wolves in 1992, the worst year on record. From 1976 to 1992 the 7,000 farms in the range reported an average of 29 livestock attacks per year—about four per 1,000 farms. In Montana from 1987 to 1992, a total of 17 cows were killed.

➤ In most wolf-populated areas, there are programs to compensate farmers and ranchers for financial losses. (Such programs are in place for both Yellowstone and New Mexico.) Total annual outlays from these programs averaged just $46,226 in Alberta, Canada, $26,922 in Minnesota, and $1,700 in Montana. Full value was paid for any lost stock.

And so the story goes—the true story. "In reality, the wolf is just another animal," concluded the federal study, and not at all the fearsome beast or evil symbol of mythology. Most New Mexicans are ready to welcome this persecuted creature back into the natural scheme of things. Yet in the hysterical anti-wolf camp, the minds are already firmly made up—and have no desire to be confused by facts.

The Snowfall

*L*azing abed in my darkened bedroom after waking on Thanksgiving morning, I was startled to hear on the radio that Santa Fe was having a major snowfall. I jumped up, ran to the window, peered through the blinds—and groaned. Sure enough, judging from the roof of my car, about six inches had fallen, and more was coming down. The radio said the snow would continue all morning and into midafternoon, then finally stop. But already it seemed enough to ruin my holiday.

I was planning to join friends out in Eldorado, 15 miles outside Santa Fe, for a jovial Thanksgiving feast. But now it seemed I would not be able to go. My car does not have four-wheel-drive, and in this year's previous snowstorm—on Election Day—I had a little skid on my way to the polling place. Risking Eldorado did not seem wise.

A can of soup and maybe a salad was about all I had in my own house, and that seemed likely to be my dinner. But I would wait and see. In the meantime, however, I had to figure out what to do about my faithful dog Max's daily walk. The plan had been to take him walking in Eldorado, with my friends' dog. Now I needed an alternative. Driving to one of our regular forest trails was out of the question. The only sensible thing was to take a stroll through the neighborhood.

In glum spirits I pulled on my high-top galoshes and a heavy coat. With snow still dumping down, out we went. At once I noted, however, that the air was mild, the snow mushy. Few cars were moving on that holiday morning, but tracks indicated that those that were out were doing OK. The storm was not as bad as it seemed.

A lone car inched by, and the driver waved. Under the circumstances, it seemed safe to let Max off his leash. Despite his advancing years, he began bounding through the snow, which is his favorite thing. At least my dog could be happy. As we passed a friend's house we stopped to say hello. She was glad to see us—the more so because her snow boots were in her car, and she had been wondering how to get them without getting her feet wet. I brought them in, she thanked me, and Max and I continued on our way.

Back on the street, a woman's car was stuck at the curb. Hearing the spinning wheels, a neighbor came out with a shovel. With a little digging and pushing we got the car out into the grooves of earlier traffic. Before she drove off, she offered to give me and Max—a stranger and a big dog—a ride. I said no thanks, we're just out for a walk in the snowstorm.

A few blocks farther along, some young boys in soggy snow forts were confronting each other across the deserted street. Happily they explained the rules of the battle about to ensue, and invited us to choose sides. I said we had to push on. As we did, one of the boys said: "My dog who died was named Max."

Dashing through the snow up ahead was a man bearing armloads of household goods from his car into a house. "A fine day I picked to move," he laughed. We exchanged names and handshakes, and I welcomed him to the neighborhood. An elderly woman had just cleared her sidewalk. "Snow is beautiful," she said, "if you like shoveling." A young fellow was trying to ski down the street, but the snow proved too mushy for that.

A little while later back home, I realized that my spirits had lifted completely. Drawing me out of my cubicle into a lovely white world, the storm had underscored why I love this town. Whether or not I went to Eldorado, the day would be just fine. And then the snow stopped, and then it melted, and then I drove to my friends' house as planned— with Max—and a good time was had by all.

The next day I read of other Santa Feans who lost their electricity or got temporarily stranded by the Thanksgiving storm. But all of them seemed to be smiling, too. Far from being the ruination of America's nicest national holiday, the snowstorm was the first gift of Christmastime.

The Silver Birds

NEWS ITEM: The Taos City Council silences protest against a planned $8 million expansion of the municipal airport, saying: "The decision has been made to build a new runway. Period." The council acknowledges that no new commercial airline has contracted to use the proposed runway, but says the expansion is designed to attract large charter planes.

NEWS ITEM: Farmington-based Mesa Airlines announces it will discontinue daily service to Taos next February, when its aircraft are upgraded from nine-passenger to 13-passenger models. "The Taos market simply cannot support the bigger aircraft," the company's marketing director explains.

NEWS ITEM: Española, 26 miles north of Santa Fe, proceeds with plans for a new airport, costing from $3.5 million to $9 million, to replace the current one. Up to 30 planes a day might use the new facility, says the airport commission chairman, and the increased traffic could give the city a financial boost.

"Mondo Cane" was the title of an offbeat movie that made a stir in the early 1960s. Loosely translated, the title means "what a peculiar world," and the film was a collection of vignettes about strange-but-true occurrences around the globe. Some of the pieces were zany, such as one about a posh pet cemetery in Hollywood. Some were poignant, such as one about giant sea turtles whose sense of direction had been altered by nuclear-bomb testing on atolls, and who could not find their way back to the ocean after laying their eggs on shore. Others fell somewhere in between.

The one that comes to mind now was about the chief of a primitive village deep in the jungles of Africa. Just as it had for centuries, his tribe was scratching out its existence from the earth. But the outside world had come close enough to sometimes overlap with the world of the chief.

From time to time he was flown by government officials in a helicopter to a modern city on the edge of the jungle, there to learn about medicine and other things that might help his people. Far more tantalizing to the chief, however, was the wealth he saw displayed on every street: cars, clothes, appliances, radios, televisions, delicious food of every kind.

Before going to the city, the chief had not realized how impoverished his people were. But now that he knew, he longed to bring them all the glittering riches he had seen. He just had to figure out how. An observant man, he noticed that at the same airport where the helicopter took him for his visits were many giant cargo craft. Being unloaded from them were huge crates full of the wondrous things he craved. He deduced that that the city man's wealth came from these big silver birds in the sky.

If only he could get those birds to come to his village, he reasoned, then his people would be rich too. Yet he could see why the airplanes did not stop in his town: They needed a big flat place to land on, and his village did not have one. Because he loved his people, the chief decided to bring the airplanes to them. He gathered the villagers and promised that if they cleared away all the trees and shrubbery from a large flat place, big silver birds would come and make everybody rich.

Thrilled by their leader's message, the people threw themselves into the task, ignoring crops, irrigation and many other things until it was finished. The work took many months. To complete the job they stacked large pyres of wood alongside the cleared strip to make bonfires, for the chief had noticed that the big birds would not come down at night unless bright lights lined the flat place.

At last everything was done. As soon as the big birds began landing, the people of the village would be poor no more. With suitable ceremony the flat place was pronounced ready. Eagerly the people awaited the arrival of the birds. They waited and waited and waited. By day and by night they took turns standing duty at the flat place, so that someone would be there to welcome the birds that would bring them wealth.

If the people neglected their former duties while waiting, that was the way it had to be. If fierce rains washed away the fertile topsoil from the stripped area, that also was the way it had to be. And if the bonfires consumed wood that might have been used for cooking or heating, well, that too had to be.

When "Mondo Cane" was filmed, a long time had passed with no birds coming down at the flat place. But the villagers still trusted their leader, still believed. The last image of the movie shows the silhouette of a lone man on duty, framed by the flames of the bonfire, while in the night sky overhead a great silver bird flies on to its destination.

Perhaps no planes have landed on that flat place yet. In any event, this little story from our peculiar world does come to mind these days.

The Severed Foot

On a warm summer day in the mid-1970s, with downtown Santa Fe full of tourists and locals, a young blond bearded man in working clothes took a toolbox to the tall stone obelisk monument in the center of the Plaza. For the next hour or so, with nobody questioning him, he carefully removed with his chisel the word "savage" from this engraved dedication: "To the heroes who have fallen in the various battles with savage Indians in the Territory of New Mexico."

Then he calmly departed. Chagrined local officials later said that he was not a city worker, as onlookers had assumed, but was apparently a nonviolent protester, making a social statement with his hammer and chisel. The man's identity was never learned—and the word "savage" was never reinscribed. Instead a plaque was mounted, semi-apologizing for its use.

Now a similar—and much more jarring— nonviolent protest has occurred. Late one night the right foot was cut off the monumental bronze statue of Spanish conquistador Don Juan de Oñate near Española. A secret group claiming responsibility for the act says it was symbolic retaliation for Oñate's order some 400 years ago to amputate the right feet of all the Acoma Pueblo warriors who were defeated by the Spaniards in an uprising.

There is much to think about here, though the thoughts are uncomfortable. Ever since its inception as a gleam in the eye of Rio Arriba County strongman Emilio Naranjo years ago, the Oñate monument has been controversial—both for its $1.2 million cost to taxpayers and for the man it commemorates. So on the eve of the quadricentennial celebration of Oñate's 1598 founding of the first European settlement in the Southwest, this brash act of vandalism heats up an ever-smoldering issue.

Oñate's admirers say he was a bold explorer, a colonizer, a technological innovator, a spreader of the Catholic faith, a large figure in history. All of this is true. His detractors say he was a ruthless conqueror, killer and enslaver of native inhabitants, and extraordinarily cruel. This too is true. Is such a man hero or monster? Obviously, it depends on whom you ask. Historians duck the question by saying that what happened happened, and should be reported and studied as fact, without value judgment. They also say men should be assessed in the context of their times, not by universal standards. But moralists say good is good and evil is evil, wherever and whenever it occurs.

Often overlooked in this unresolvable debate is another adage: that history is written by the winners. Jack Collum, a puckish poet friend in Colorado, contemplated all the hoo-rah directed at the Columbus Quincentenary in

1992 and asked this question: "Didja ever see a headline 'HITLER DISCOVERS POLAND'?"

And actually, the question is a good one. Without a doubt, if the other side had won World War II, we'd be seeing statues of Hitler and Tojo everywhere, and would be taught in school that they were among the greatest men of all time. Throughout the former Soviet Union were monumental statues of the butcher Lenin, but they all came tumbling down when communism did.

Don Juan de Oñate was on the winning side in Southwestern history. Thus his fans and descendants have always considered him a hero. Yet history has undergone substantial re-evaluation in recent times. Though one of the boldest visionaries ever, and truly a shaper of the world, Columbus left such a legacy of plunder and horror that his historical star has dimmed, and the holiday named for him is fading from the American scene. A recent book on John Kennedy virtually strips him of respect. And so should Oñate be held up to tough scrutiny, as well as homage. His achievements were large, and will be remembered. But amputating feet is a hideous outrage in any age or epoch.

The people who erected the Santa Fe Plaza obelisk in 1868 felt justified in insulting Indians as "savage." But when the word was removed a century later, it was excused, not replaced. Perhaps Oñate's bronze foot should be left off permanently, and a plaque installed to explain its absence. Then pilgrims to his shrine can absorb both his grandeur and his horror, in some form of truth.

Postscript: The foot severed from the Oñate statue was never recovered. A replacement foot, cast from the statue's mold, was attached within days of the incident, which took place in the autumn of 1998. A protective fence was also installed around the monument, which now is locked at night.

The Movies

*T*he recently announced plans for a 14-screen, state-of-the-art movie multiplex on the south side of town brought this writer a rush of memories about the "bad old days" of film-going in Santa Fe. And lemme tell you: They were BAD.

When I arrived in 1971, Santa Fe had just two indoor theaters, the Lensic and the El Paseo, practically next-door to each other downtown on San Francisco Street. On Cerrillos Road were two drive-ins, the Yucca and the Pueblo. In the Pen Road strip mall was an X-rated house. St. John's College had an art-film program on weekends. And that was just about it.

But the scarcity of screens was only the beginning of Santa Fe's film woes back then. Both downtown screens and one drive-in were run by the small Commonwealth Theaters group, which treated this city like an unwanted, unloved stepchild. Most movies shown here were B-grade clunkers that few of us had ever heard of. The occasional major title that found its way to town would arrive months or even a year or two after its national release—presumably because booking it so late was cheaper. I filed away reviews from magazines and the Albuquerque papers, to remind me what such movies were about when and if they ever came.

On the occasions when I did go to a movie, I often wished I hadn't. The prints usually were scratchy, streaked and spliced, from being old and used. But the worst thing of all was Commonwealth's custom of stopping films in midstream—often in mid-sentence—at the end of a reel, to impose a false popcorn break on the audience. It was enough to ruin a movie. Every movie house in the country had figured out by the 1930s how to synchronize reels to give an uninterrupted show. But Commonwealth pretended it didn't have the technology to do that. At one film that jarred to a halt midway, an audience member, obviously a stranger to town, cried out: "I can't believe this!" Someone else replied: "Welcome to Santa Fe!"

The drive-ins also showed out-of-date films, and closed down for the winter. Fleeing to St. John's College didn't help much, either. Although the movies were well chosen, visibility was terrible in the flat-floored Great Hall, and the students would try to impress each other by making loud, annoying quips to the actors onscreen. Believe it or not, I never checked out the X-rated place.

Some slight relief came when Commonwealth opened the two-screen Coronado Twin in the Cordova Road shopping center and shut down the El Paseo. But this little duplex was so flimsily constructed that sounds from one movie could be heard in the other hall, as could noise from the bowling alley overhead. And these brand-new theaters kept up the false intermissions.

The local movie scene did not really begin to improve until a maverick independent named Ralph Lindell opened a two-screen house at De Vargas Mall in 1974. Bidding fiercely for first-run movies, and also booking innovative filmfests and film classics requested by his audience, he finally brought Santa Fe into the modern movie era. And the movies he showed did NOT have phony intermissions. Facing competition at last, Commonwealth cleaned up its act as well. And though Lindell eventually sold out to his rival, things never reverted to the bad old ways.

The rest of the 1970s and then the 1980s brought more improvements. The most significant was the opening of the Collective Fantasy (in the theater now named the Jean Cocteau) by a brave young group of idealists determined to give Santa Fe its first true art-film house. An array of foreign-language and low-budget independent films, too small to be of interest to the big boys, added delicious richness to the local mix.

Today ours is a terrific movie town, with some two dozen screens, long-run current releases, art theaters, ambitious offbeat programs, an annual festival and more. And soon, perhaps, a new multiplex. But lemme tell you— we didn't always have it so good.

The War Correspondent

At a small white house in a tiny hamlet on the utterly flat plains of Indiana, one of the most beloved men ever to live in New Mexico was honored, yet again, one April day in 1995. Ernie Pyle was his name, and if you cannot quite place it, it is because you are too young. Any American who remembers World War II, which was sweeping to its conclusion half a century ago, will not forget the name Ernie Pyle.

He was a war correspondent, the best there ever was. Sharing foxholes and cigarettes and fear with ordinary GIs, he told their story as it had never been told before—from the mud up. *Here Is Your War*, a book-length collection of his dispatches, gave pride and heart to America's mothers and fathers and brothers and sisters and sweethearts, waiting and praying for their faraway *Brave Men*—the title of another of his books.

Like so many of the soldiers whose tales he told, Pyle died in combat. On April 18, 1945, a Japanese sniper on Ie Shima, a 10-square-mile island in the North Pacific, sent three bullets into his head. He was buried there, and atop his grave, American soldiers placed a simple plaque. "On this spot," it read, "the 77th Infantry Division lost a buddy, Ernie Pyle." His death, announced to the nation by a sorrowful President Harry Truman, was mourned in every state—but was felt most keenly in two, Indiana and New Mexico.

A proud but restless Hoosier, Pyle was born in 1900 in the farming village of Dana—where the 50-year mark of his passing was commemorated in the recent ceremony. It was a grand occasion, with a crowd estimated at anywhere from the high hundreds to the low thousands, legions of them grayed and grizzled ex-GIs. At the center of the site stood a modest, white, wooden home, the house where Pyle was born.

Deserted for a decade, decaying, the house was resurrected in 1976, as part of America's Bicentennial. Lifted onto wheels in the field where it was rotting, it was pulled to a new site just off the main road to Dana—U.S. 36, the Ernie Pyle Memorial Highway. Now the house itself is also a memorial and a museum, which each year draws some 15,000 visitors, one of whom has been this writer.

Those of us who call New Mexico home have a special reason to make this journey, for Pyle also called New Mexico home. After wandering constantly for years, he and his wife, Jerry, chose at last to settle in Albuquerque. The foundation of their house was laid in 1940, as German bombs began to fall on London, where Ernie quickly was dispatched, to cover the Blitz, his first war assignment.

New Mexicans passing through the homespun museum of the Indiana birthplace—as '40s-vintage songs of the Ink Spots, Eddy Howard, the young Sinatra, play softly in the background—find many reminders of Pyle's links to his adopted state. There is the watch presented to him in 1944 by Mayor Clyde Tingley and the citizens of Albuquerque; the January 1942 issue of *New Mexico Magazine,* in which he explained "Why Albuquerque"; a videotape of a black-and-white tourism film called "Ernie Pyle's New Mexico"; two volumes of letters to his friend E. J. Shaffer, editor of the *Albuquerque Tribune;* mementos from his final home, which he loved but barely got to know. He and his wife had no children, and when she died, not long after Ernie, the house was willed to the city of Albuquerque, which now runs it as the Ernie Pyle Memorial Library.

The *Santa Fe Reporter* and I also have a link to Ernie Pyle, I am glad to say. He was one of my boyhood heroes, and when I had my own newspaper to run, I arranged with the Scripps Howard Foundation, which holds his copyrights, to print one of his columns each week. The ones we used were not from the battlefield but were instead his lovely *Home Country* celebrations of pre-war America, from the years he was a vagabond correspondent roaming the land with his wife. Thus the *Reporter* became the only newspaper in the country still publishing him, which led one reader to muse: "What a strange paper—your best writer has been dead 40 years."

From Ernie's wider life the souvenirs in the house in Dana, Indiana, are more dramatic: a gray tweed jacket with the elbows worn away, the only civilian coat he could find when Eleanor Roosevelt invited him to the White

House; his portrait from the cover of *Time*; his foxhole typewriter; the telegram of his death, sent to his parents by U.S. Navy Secretary James Forrestal; the flag from his casket. And outside the house, dedicated in the 1995 ceremony, stand two authentic World War II-era Quonset huts, never used. Found forgotten in a Rhode Island naval yard, they were sent to Dana, to become fitting monuments to Ernie Pyle's legacy.

The wars that followed 1945 never produced another Ernie Pyle. More cynical, less meaningful, the conflicts in Korea, Vietnam, the Persian Gulf, Latin America, generated either a muzzled form of journalism or—depressingly often —reports of futility and atrocities, such as Vietnam's My Lai massacre. But half a century ago, one small, scared man with a typewriter—a man who still can make Indianans, New Mexicans and all Americans proud—moved a soldier's wife to write when she learned that he had died: "I knew him not, but I loved him."

The Lonesome Place

If you want to be alone, go to the Bisti Badlands.
There the outside world does not intrude. And barely
exists. There you will be by yourself, and seldom if ever
will you have felt so much so. The Bisti Badlands are in
Navajo country, in northwestern New Mexico, south of
Farmington and north of Gallup, off a back-country state
highway numbered 371. You don't get there by accident.
Very few get there at all.

Almost nothing grows in the Bisti, and nothing has
been built there, except a rough dirt road and a thin wire
fence. The Badlands combine isolation with desolation, in
as pure a mixture of both as you will find. If you find it.

The Badlands, which officially were designated the
Bisti Wilderness Area by Congress in 1984, are a grimly
beautiful region of interbedded shale, sandstone and coal,
fashioned by erosion into a landscape that might return in
your nightmares.

The dominant shape is flat. The dominant color is
gray. But strange red hills pop up here and there, purple

swirls decorate the earth, craggy black formations are etched against the sky. Dark stripes of coal run horizontal in the fine gray sand. Little piles of brown rocks are scattered through the Badlands, broken down by the patient crush of time. In just a few spots, gravel patches boldly display most of the hues of the rainbow. The sky above is usually blue, with clouds of white on many days. At night it all turns black.

And the dominant sound is silence. The voices of people passing through get swallowed by it, while the unaccompanied visitor hears nothing but the crunch of his footsteps—and sometimes, especially in the spring, the wind. The Badlands get blistering hot in summer, bone-numbing cold in winter. Except after an infrequent storm, or when snow lies on the ground, you will search in vain for water. Vegetation is limited to tough little weeds and a low, crinkly ground cover, adding spots of green to nature's harsh palette.

Life is scarce in the Bisti. A pair of crows may fly overhead, a lizard may dart underfoot. But there is nothing to graze on, nothing to drink, no shelter from the sun. Not even a coyote can make a living there. It is not called the Badlands for nothing. The Bisti is not really a spectacular place—just an exceptionally different place.

And a few wanderers do come, to know this barren outback for themselves. They are a hardy bunch, and certainly persistent, for getting there is tricky. From the north, some 40 miles of scrub desert separate the Bisti from modern civilization. From the south, it's more like 70. A roadside marker indicates where to turn off from Highway 371, but after that it's pretty much up to you. The gray dirt road heading east pounds your car with washboard ruts; and frequent unmarked intersections leave you unsure whether you're on the right track, or if you'll remember the way out.

A couple of windswept ruins are the only man-built structures on the road to the Bisti Badlands. Just 3,946 acres bear the title Bisti Wilderness. Environmentalists wanted more, but the coal in the region caused mining companies to oppose the designation; and Congress, as usual, compromised. The flimsy wire fence marks the official boundary, and "No Trespassing" signs warn you off the property of the surrounding Idaho-based mining firm.

Inside the fence, however, is a tiny world apart, where you are free to roam. Tramping through the Bisti's hills and washes, flatlands and low mesas, coal seams and bedrock, will not take long—just an hour or two, maybe a little more if you get turned around. But unless your car breaks down, in which case you'll be in trouble, you'll get out all right.

Then you will be one of the few who know the Bisti Badlands. More than anything else, you will know it is out there in the lonesome. All by itself.

The Cave

*L*ooking for adventure, young Jim Kennicott, a student at North Hollywood High School in California, worked on a U. S. Interior Department surveying crew in the summers of 1944 and '45. Both years he lived in tents in remote areas of Arizona's San Francisco Mountains, north of Flagstaff. And in one of those years, he is not sure which, he stumbled upon a cave.

Hidden in a yellow pine forest, the cave at first glance seemed merely a collapsed crater, about 100 feet in diameter, left by some ancient volcanic event. But at its bottom, 15 or 20 feet down, was a hole large enough for humans to enter. Intrigued, Kennicott and some buddies decided to explore that hole. With flashlights and a ball of string to mark their way, half a dozen of them slipped into its darkness one bright weekend day, while one guy stayed on top in case of trouble.

Near the entrance they found an old bottle or two, signs that long-gone pioneers might have camped there. In the next chambers they found the droppings of bats and either a bobcat or mountain lion. This gave them pause, but they pressed on.

The going got rough. Several times they crawled through tiny passageways on their stomachs. Then the cave opened onto rooms 30 or 40 feet long, tall enough for walking. Crystal-clear water dripped in some of the rooms, and the air was cool and crisp. But no sign of human or animal life could be seen.

The explorers were scared all the way. What if the cave fell in? What if they got lost, or fell off a ledge, or got a foot stuck? What if they were jumped by a big cat, with no room to turn or flee? Claustrophobia hung heavy upon them. Yet on they went. After what seemed like at least a mile, however, they could go no farther. The crawlway tapered down to a fissure barely large enough for a hand. So they scratched their names and the date into the moist clay lining the cave at that place, and crawled back to surface.

In the early 1950s Kennicott attended the University of California at Los Angeles. There he told two of his Phi Delta Theta fraternity brothers about the cave, and they wanted to see it for themselves. Finding it again proved surprisingly easy, and everybody squeezed his way to the end. The newcomers put their names and that of their fraternity next to the earlier ones. Then for 40 years Kennicott forgot about the cave.

After college he went to work for an insurance company, rising to division manager. He lived in several places, but on his first trip to New Mexico he knew he wanted to retire here. He bought a lot in Santa Fe, and when he reached his 60s a few years ago, he left his job and began building his dream house. Up to his ears in construction, Kennicott was startled one day by a letter sent to his Santa Fe address by a ranger in Flagstaff. The U. S. Forest Service had just discovered the cave, the ranger said. Could Kennicott tell them more about it?

Untouched in the stillness, the names from almost half a century ago had been found. And the name of the fraternity. From Phi Delta Theta's national office the ranger got the current addresses of Kennicott and his friends. And now, under the mandate of the 1988 Federal Cave Resources Protection Act, the government wanted to learn all it could.

The ranger's letter asked many questions: How did Kennicott find the cave? Was he aware of other caves in the area? Who were the other people whose names were there? What artifacts were found? Were bats or other animals present? Were any photos taken? The letter's most amazing line, however, revealed that the cave was only 900 feet long. In memory, it still stretched on for a mile.

When his astonishment subsided, Kennicott sent a lengthy reply. In time the ranger wrote again: "Concerning the cave, it is our intention to conserve it much as it was when you visited so many years ago." Trips to it would be carefully restricted.

"When you read about the early days—John Wesley Powell and those other guys who mapped the West for the first time—you never think your life will be anything like that," Kennicott says, smiling broadly in his retirement home. "But this does have a historical perspective to it, doesn't it?"

The Sweatlodge

A sense of nervous apprehension infused the
dozen-plus people who converged Saturday morning on
the parking lot of DeVargas Mall in Santa Fe, and then
caravaned north to the tiny village of La Madera and the
sprawling old adobe home of Jicarilla Apache potter Felipe
Ortega. But there, sitting in a circle, telling why they had
come, they loosened.

"Last year I almost died from AIDS," said the first
man. "Right now I'm better, but I get so tired of taking all
those medications." A woman followed: "In 1994 I was
diagnosed with acute leukemia and told I had 30 to 90
days to live. But here I am." Others in the ring were facing
cancer, either metastasized or in remission; depression;
the death of a husband; more AIDS. Five members of the
group were caregivers. I came as a writer.

The assembly was the August getaway of Earth
Walks for Health, a Santa Fe-based program that in the
years since its beginning in 1994 has sought—according to
its mission statement—"to assist people facing serious

health challenges gain additional options in dealing with their illness through an organized exploration of the values, arts, lifeways and earth wisdom teachings of traditional cultures of the Southwest."

The program is modest in size, no more than 20 participants for each of the May-through-October monthly events. It is modest in cost, just $30 per person, including two generous meals. It is also modest in its claims, boasting no miraculous cures from bringing illness and ancient healing face-to-face. But Doug Conwell, the therapist and counselor who directs Earth Walks for Health, rules nothing out. "We've had people tell us the weekend changed their lives," he says. "We have people still alive now who were expected to be dead a long time ago."

The outings, usually with a Saturday overnight, tap into Hispanic, Native American and Mexican indigenous healing. Drum makers, *curanderas*, naturopaths, farmers, storytellers and dream healers, among others, have taught their ways. The centerpiece of this particular weekend was a traditional Jicarilla Apache sweatlodge.

But that climactic event, scheduled for moonrise, was preceded by "medicine circles," a relaxed lunch during which we all talked easily with one another, and then a hike into a dazzling pink-granite canyon, to a gentle river in which some of us swam. We also slipped off to a stone altar, where a white-bearded Anglo man spoke to us in the channeled voice of a "medicine grandmother."

At nightfall our host instructed us in the protocol of the sweatlodge, behind his sprawling home. The sweatlodge—from time out of memory an element of the culture and religion of indigenous people of the American

Southwest and many other parts of the world. The sweatlodge ritual is a purification technique, to align body, mind and spirit. Some sweatlodge ceremonies are so sacred that only tribal members may enter. Others, like this one, admit visitors.

For many hours head-sized stones are heated in a fire until they glow red-hot. Then they are carried, carefully, to a pit dug in the earth inside the lodge. In some cultures the dome-shaped lodge is built of saplings, in others bamboo. The one behind Ortega's house was made of mud and logs, covered by tarpaulins to hold in the heat

A lodge has no windows or other openings, to let in even the light of the blackest night. The low door closes tight. The ceiling is not high enough for standing, only sitting or lying. The first blast of heat inside is penetrating, astonishing—some would say stifling. Then the heat gets only more intense, as four times during the ceremony water is poured onto the stones to make steam, and three times fresh red-hot stones are added to the pit.

The moment that we on the Earth Walk both feared and keenly anticipated had come. Most of us, men and women, crawled naked into the low, round lodge, pitch-dark except for the dull glow of the stones. But the modesty of clothing was all right, too, and a few of the participants chose it. When the circle filled, the door closed. Then the first pail of water was poured, and the black heat, sweat and intensity bored in upon us.

One participant knew at once that this was not the place for her. She called out to leave, which also was all right. Then for two searing hours, the group confronted its demons. In heat and steam and profusive sweat, the lodge rang with remorse and fear and courage and acceptance and beauty and defiance and valor. Cancer cells were commanded to die. Cries escaped from broken hearts. Ancestors and memories were evoked. Every participant crawled out drained in body, euphoric in spirit, and connected with everyone who had shared the superheated darkness.

After the sweatlodge came showers, cold or warm, depending on the taker. Then a feast, then sleep, then a big breakfast, then a final circle, then the road home. A young surveyor diagnosed with terminal testicular cancer rode with me in my car. He said he was determined to beat the cancer, but was still making provisions for his wife. Both he and she were scared, he said.

I do not know if such weekends can help overcome the hideous challenges we all face, now or somewhere down the road. But I do feel sure that days spent with Earth Walks for Health will not be subtracted from the sum of any life.

The Magdalena Playhouse

*B*efore she left for the New York City stage, before she took her acting career to London, before she married there and had a daughter and became a British citizen, before she herded sheep in Wyoming and Montana, living in solitude for months in a tiny trailer shack, before she established her avant-garde theater in Salt Lake City, and long before she relocated that venture to dusty Magdalena, New Mexico, Donna Todd attended Tucker High School with me, in a little country town in Georgia.

But that was long ago and far away—and the story I wish to tell today is the current one. I was on the road last week and caught up with my old friend in Magdalena, New Mexico, 27 miles west of Socorro, a little east of the Plains of San Agustin.

Stage-struck since childhood, Donna knew always that her future lay in the theater. It didn't take her long to get from Georgia to New York, and from there to London, where she lived 10 years and picked up a British accent that has not gone away. In England she was semi-successful, appearing in several productions, starring in a few, earning enough to live on but too little to get ahead—a familiar tale to many performers.

The other call she heard all through the years came from the American West. For several summers she went from England to the American mountains up north, to tend flocks of sheep and read at night. In time her marriage ended and her London career seemed stuck. So she decided to return stateside and start her own theater. Circumstances brought her to Salt Lake City, where she and a partner founded the London Frontier Theatre Company in 1991. For two years it struggled, producing original works, gaining marvelous reviews, and drawing barely subsistence audiences from that extremely conservative Western metropolis.

In 1993 their operation coasted to a halt. Donna felt that Santa Fe might be fertile ground for reviving it, and so she moved here, living three months in a downscale Cerrillos Road motel. She and I reconnected then for the first time in 30 years. But Santa Fe was not the answer. Dismayed by the high cost of everything here, Donna saw she had no hope of starting a new theater with just a small inheritance from her mother. So she kept looking, farther and farther out, but still in New Mexico.

Las Vegas, 60 miles south of Santa Fe, did not seem quite right, either, although Donna did live more than a year in a small trailer halfway between here and there. I would visit, and she would talk about Magdalena. A town of 800 souls and empty buildings galore from its mining heyday, it seemed receptive to people with ideas— like Donna. In 1996 she moved there and bought two buildings, one to live in, one to rent out for income. That pretty much wiped out her inheritance, so all she had left for grubstaking her theater was spunk. Alone except for some faithful mutts, she began meeting locals and telling them of her plans.

The resuscitated London Frontier Theatre Company made its Magdalena debut in 1996, as part of the village's Old-Timers Days celebration. The premiere production was "Stagecoach to Decameron," a Westernized take on Boccaccio's 14th-century road saga. Held in the town's senior center, it sold out both nights.

"Long Road, Free Wind: True Histories of Frontier Women" followed in the autumn. It also packed the house, and there was even a performance 26 miles away in the much larger town of Socorro. As with "Stagecoach" the script was original, written by Donna—no royalties to pay that way.

Her little theater adds extra dimension to the term "non-profit corporation." It has no fixed performance site, although Donna did make a token—and unsuccessful—$1 bid for an old Depression-era gym built by the WPA and now fading under the Magdalena sun. Her personal finances are just as tight, as she chooses monthly between electric and telephone bills.

Yet proud Magdalena is one New Mexico town that has its own professional-caliber theater. In 1997 London Frontier presented an original Valentine special, based on the wicked wit and urbane world of 1920s "Algonquin Table" writer Dorothy Parker. The stage this time was in a Main Street cafe, where dinner and the play cost $25 per couple. A steady stream of plays has flowed since then, the audiences keep coming, and the theater has received grants from foundations and the state.

My childhood friend has wandered much and gone a long way from Tucker, Georgia. But pausing in her brave new world, I knew she came to the right place, which now has been touched by a star.

The Henchman

*T*he fledgling *Santa Fe Reporter* was barely a year old in 1975, and as its editor I was looking into the hyper-excited eyes of our young film critic, Ken Ausubel. "I tell you he's here in town," Ken told me. "John Erhlichman has moved to Santa Fe!"

John Ehrlichman: one of the most notorious men in America. A ringleader of the notorious Watergate scandal in Washington, he was fired from the Nixon White House shortly before the president himself resigned in disgrace in 1974. John Erhlichman —who now has died, at the age of 73.

Although Ken Ausubel has distinguished himself in many ways since then, he was kind of a wild-eyed kid at that time. His Erhlichman sighting strained a prudent editor's credulity. "How did you find out?" I asked. "How do you know it's him?"

"I saw him outside his house," Ken insisted. "I recognized him from his photos, even though he's grown a beard." The beard gave me pause. Any man looks different behind one. I was not convinced. I told Ken to check it out. If he pinned it down, the *Reporter* would break the story. If not, we wouldn't.

So Ken staked out Ehrlichman's house. After several days of seeing a furtive young man with a camera skulking about in the bushes, Ehrlichman grew weary of the game. Assuming that his "stalker" was from the town's daily paper, Erhlichman marched down to *The New Mexican*. "Yes, I've moved to Santa Fe," he told a startled editor. "Yes, you can say so in the paper. But no, I don't want to talk about it—no interviews. Now, please call off your bird dog who's been bugging me all week long."

Thus the *Reporter* lost what should have been one of its earliest big scoops. But our Ehrlichman connection only started there. Another *Reporter* writer, Frank Clifford, now with the *Los Angeles Times*, contacted Ehrlichman quietly. Both privacy and the news were important, Frank said—and when the time was right, he hoped Erhlichman would talk to Santa Fe's weekly.

Before that time came, however, Ehrlichman made another link with the *Reporter*. Under the pen name "Agricola" he began submitting occasional guest columns, full of details about obscure, mismanaged federal programs in Washington. As editor, I didn't think his topics related much to Santa Fe—but I relished our little secret, and I happily published all his pieces.

On this cordial footing, Erhlichman gave his first major post-Watergate interview to Clifford and the *Reporter*, in May 1976. It was big news at the time. We called it "The Ehrlichman Version." I pulled strings to place it on the *Washington Post/LA Times/Newsday* syndicated wire, and newspapers all over America ran it.

Ehrlichman's words were guarded and self-serving, as could be expected. Then he spent 18 months in federal prison.

When he got out, Erhlichman returned to Santa Fe. As editor I had maintained an arm's-length distance from this half-famous, half-infamous man, and I did not seek him out. He was writing books now, not anonymous columns. But he did keep making news.

And so, our paths crossed once more. A 1982 book-signing at Fenn Gallery in Santa Fe for *Witness to Power*, Ehrlichman's personal take on Watergate, was covered for the *Reporter* by writer Steve Terrell, who later moved on to *The New Mexican*. Steve's account was objective, but it mentioned some protesters who came to the event and told Ehrlichman: "Making money from crime is perverted." Then we published a letter to the editor that blasted Ehrlichman's "lies" and his "country club prison."

Shortly afterward, Ehrlichman spoke at a dinner event in Santa Fe. I went with an old friend of his, a woman who had attended Christian Scientist church with him in his hometown of Seattle. He ate at our table, and was as friendly to me as could be. But stepping to the podium, he launched a vicious attack on me, the *Reporter* and Steve Terrell—for words that had been written not in the article but in the letter to the editor!

From my chair I pointed out his error, in a voice for the room to hear. He angrily insisted that the offending words had come not from the letter but from Terrell's article. "Look it up," I responded from my seat. "Look it up." A few days later he sent me a bristly note of apology, still mad at the *Reporter*. "You were right and I was wrong," he conceded. "But your story was still lousy." He and I never met again.

After a while Ehrlichman left town, lived elsewhere for years, and now has died. But for a while he certainly enlivened the life of Santa Fe—and my own.

The Homeboy

Gilbert was always gentle around me. But years ago, I am told, he got into a fistfight with a man who fell down, struck his head on the curb, and died. Gilbert then "cleaned himself up, cut his hair, put on a three-piece suit" and stood trial for involuntary manslaughter. He was acquitted on all charges.

Now Gilbert himself is dead. He was found lying face-down in 18 inches of water in a culvert near the intersection of Cerrillos Road and St. Francis Drive. Undoubtedly he was drunk when he fell. Gilbert was almost always drunk.

Gilbert was a neighbor, who lived two doors away from me in the South Capitol part of Santa Fe. The area is quite old, but has become increasingly gentrified in recent years. But not Gilbert's place, a rundown structure that long ago was a general store. In an open area between that house and mine, Gilbert and his friends would often gather and talk, and drink beer, wine and liquor. Sometimes visitors asked me if I was bothered by the unkempt spectacle. I answered no, not at all. They were here long before I came. I hope they are not bothered by me.

I moved in several years ago, and soon made the acquaintance of Gilbert, his brother, some cousins and their friends. We did not have much in common, but there was no reason not to get along. Some of the guys were quite sociable, but talking with Gilbert was hard. Through his intoxication he mumbled, slurred and had difficulty stringing words into sentences.

Yet there was an innate friendliness about him. He had a big grin that brightened his face, despite the fact that most of his teeth were gone. He was a tall, thin man with a shambling walk, dirty long black hair and a face ravaged by the booze. I wondered how he kept going, how he stayed alive. He just did.

A while back he started knocking on my door from time to time, to ask if I could help him out with some spare change. I thought about that and decided I could. The parameters of his life were narrow, and not much good happened within them. If a dollar or two from me could provide a little cheer, then good for us both. But when he began coming around two or three times a week, I told him that it was too frequent. Gilbert was not offended. I never saw him angry. After that, it was twice a month or so. Now and then he asked for rides to places he needed to go. Other times I would see him on the street and give him a lift. He would sit in the car and chuckle at some inward merriment, and give me a handshake and a "Thanks, neighbor" at ride's end.

Returning from a trip last week, I was saddened to hear of Gilbert's death. On Sunday I walked over to his place, where his brother and some friends were drinking beer. I joined them. We talked about Gilbert, and I learned things I hadn't known.

He was only 46, though he looked much older. He had two sons. He was kind of wild as a youth, but had been peaceful now for many years. He lived his whole life in Santa Fe, and has an extended family here. His nickname was "Tater," because of all the vodka he drank. Vodka is distilled from potatoes.

A fellow in the group who learned barbering in prison—"going there was the best thing that ever happened to me"—had cut Gilbert's hair and bathed him now and then. A lifelong buddy remembered their childhood. I was told about the manslaughter trial.

A sister of Gilbert's drove up and got mad about the gathering. "This is a time for mourning, not partying," she said. Gilbert's brother replied, "We're having a wake for him." The sister left, still angry, and the brother said, "Dying is just a natural part of living. It's all part of the same thing"

Later that day I went to the Palace of the Governors, to participate in a gathering for Santa Fe's Living Treasures program, which celebrates lives that have made an enormous contribution to the city. A most impressive collection of people was there. But back home, I felt sad again about my neighbor Gilbert. He too was a Santa Fean, and he too made a contribution

The Low and the Mighty

*T*win scourges have afflicted Santa Fe in recent times, and both are eroding what has made this place so special. Those scourges are the lowlifes and the highlifes.

The lowlifes are the criminals, who rob and rape, assault and mug. The highlifes are the people who build their showcase homes on hillsides and ridgetops. Though their methods of destruction are completely different, the damage done by both groups is equal.

A lowlife is someone who does not care about the rights of others. When one of them wants something, he takes it: skulking through a broken-into house, accosting tourists on the street, attacking a woman in her bed—or in her office. What matters to these people is to gratify their own needs. The needs or feelings of others do not count.

A highlife—who may be an exemplary citizen in every other way—brings a similar attitude to his house. If he wants a magnificent view, then by God, he wants a view. It does not matter that, almost by definition, his home on high must be looked at by everybody down below.

This is private property! When it comes to a man's castle, the feelings of others do not count.

Like all cities, Santa Fe has always had a criminal element and, I suppose, a certain number of self-important homeowners. But lately these twin scourges have grown to epidemic proportions, threatening the stability, the peace of mind, the very identity of the community.

The lowlifes have established a climate of fear that undermines Santa Fe's economic base, tourism. They have made visitors and residents alike apprehensive about going out and coming in. They have made us worried about walking our own streets. Their acts of violence have wounded many people.

But what about a raped hillside? Is that not also an act of violence? What about the thousands and thousands of Santa Fe souls that wilt a little more each time they look toward the mountains, only to see yet another once-lovely ridge devastated by yet another mansion that screams down at the town: "Look at me—I am a BIG SHOT!"

Before the rise of the twin scourges, Santa Fe was a place where people got along better than they do now. It was a place close to nature, sheltered by ancient, inviolate foothills stretching on into the distant mountains. Like the sun and the sky, the hills belonged to everyone. The town was then an unpretentious place, where state workers, heiresses, woodcutters and retirees lived side by side, and liked it that way. It all was part of what made Santa Fe special.

The rich and the poor found graceful ways to coexist in those days. Wealthy Santa Feans did fabulous things behind the adobe walls of their homes, but left the exteriors plain, so as not to jar the neighborhood. Or they tucked their homes into valleys, or surrounded them with trees, or built them off in the country. Ostentatious displays were snickered down.

But that was back when taste and sensitivity were more important than ego, back before "In your face!" and "If you got it, flaunt it" became dueling national mottos on opposite ends of the economic spectrum, before violence was glorified on television, along with "Lifestyles of the Rich and Famous."

Longer than most American communities, Santa Fe held out against these forces. But lately they have found us—and the discovery has not been pretty. More and more, those who can afford it are swarming up the hillsides, California-style, with their statement homes; while down below, state workers and woodcutters, and their children, are reminded daily that the town they took for granted is slipping away from them. Nor are they the only ones who mourn the ravaged hills.

Between the lowlifes and the highlifes, the rest of us are squeezed. They both should stop what they are doing. The lowlifes must learn there are peaceful ways to interact with other human beings. The highlifes must learn there are discreet sites for their homes. It is all a matter of respect.

Let's try again to get along. Let's turn back to the old ways. Let's pray that both the highlifes and the lowlifes see and cease the damage they are doing to the special place that Santa Fe has been, and still might remain.

The Christmas Confession

Confession is said to be good for the soul, especially around Christmastime—and besides, I'm certain that the statute of limitations has run out by now. So at last I can tell a dark, deep secret: I once cheated the post office out of its due.

It happened years ago, in the holiday season. I was sending out Christmas cards. (Yes, I actually do that, so as not to lose touch with those who might otherwise vanish into the mist.) And I was quite unhappy with the cost of the postage stamps, which had just sustained another maddening increase—up to 23 cents, or 27, or whatever it was back then.

With hazy childhood memories of a three-cent first-class stamp (yes, that's how old I am)—and a distinct adult recollection of someone saying, "Can you believe that it now costs eight cents to mail a letter!"—I was in a Scrooge-like mood as I contemplated my card list and calculated the postal toll. It was enough to drain my cheer. And then I had an inspiration!

Yes! Yes! I just knew it would work. It had the simplicity of genius. But first there must be a test run. I telephoned a friend in Los Alamos and drew her into the conspiracy. Then I mailed her a holiday card. But instead of putting her address in the normal place—centered on the front of the envelope—I put it in the upper-left, return-address spot. I put my own name and address in the middle. And when the card went out, it bore no stamp.

The very next day, she reported back. Bingo! The card had been delivered to her house, imprinted with a message in bold black letters: "RETURNED FOR POSTAGE." The scheme had worked! My card had gone through just as planned—and all for free. I was beside myself: at last a way, a foolproof way, to beat the high cost of mailing.

Quickly I did some arithmetic, rounded off to make it easy. If I sent 100 cards using this system, I could save $23 (or $27 or whatever the price of stamps was back then) on the current Christmas season, then more and more each year. After a while, that could start adding up to real money.

But why limit such a brilliant plan to Christmas cards? There was no reason it would not work equally well on any kind of mail, all through the year. I checked my financial records. Already that year I had spent $378 on business mail alone, and something less than half that amount on personal postage. By converting totally to the new system, I could save a fortune.

Visions of riches began dancing in my head. With, say, $500 in sneaked postage the first year, then maybe $650 the next, as I grew more adroit with the scheme, and then who-knew-what in subsequent years, as the price of stamps kept rising and rising and rising—clearly, the sky itself was the limit. I pictured all these savings going into mutual funds, or compound-interest certificates of deposit, or even government bonds. Then year after year the yield would just keep growing and growing.

Who among us has not wished that miraculously one day we might be given, in one lump sum, all the loose change we threw over the years at candy bars, or movies, or airport hot dogs, or photos that we never looked at again? It sure does add up.

So here I was, on the verge of my big breakthrough. Today the post office, tomorrow the gas company, finally the world. One by one, I would slip past our common adversaries. To dash through without a hand laid on me—it was a glorious vision.

But suddenly I lost my nerve. Though my Los Alamos friend shared my delight in the ruse, I worried about other Christmas correspondents. Reconciled to the real world, they might not see the beauty. Nor might book and magazine editors, or agents, or distant journalists or others I wrote to. Some of them might even think less of me for doing it. And if I called them to explain, the phone bill would quickly exceed the saved postage. It all was getting awkward.

And then there was the grim specter of federal prison.

In the end, my great scam died aborning. All I ever saved was 23 cents for one stamp. Or was it 27? Now I grumpily send 37-cent cards, like anybody else. But my idea is still genius—and for just $5 sent to me in a plain brown envelope, you can try it, too. (Surely that statute of limitations has expired.)

*N*ow a free-lance writer, Richard McCord was for more than 25 years a journalist in New York and New Mexico. In 1974 he founded the weekly *Santa Fe Reporter*, and was for 14 years its editor and co-publisher. His work has been honored by the New Mexico Press Association and the Albuquerque Press Club, and on the national level by the Scripps Howard Foundation, the National Press Club, the National Newspaper Association, Investigative Reporters and Editors, and with a runner-up citation for the Pulitzer Prize. His 1996 book *The Chain Gang: One Newspaper versus the Gannett Empire* placed second for the Mott Award for the best book about journalism that year.

Printed in the United States
21232LVS00007BA/337-360